Philosophy as Criticism

Philosophy as Criticism

*Essays on Dennett, Searle, Foot,
Davidson, Nozick*

İLHAM DİLMAN

Edited by Brian Davies
and
Mario von der Ruhr

continuum

The Continuum International Publishing Group
80 Maiden Lane, New York, NY 10038
The Tower Building, 11 York Road, London SE1 7NX

www.continuumbooks.com

Library of Congress Cataloging-in-Publication Data
A catalog record for this book is available from the Library of Congress.

ISBN: HB: 978-1-4411-9249-3
          PB: 978-1-4411-4691-5

Typeset by Pindar NZ, Auckland, New Zealand
Printed and bound in the United States of America

Contents

Editorial Preface

Ilham Dilman died of cancer on 17 January 2003. During his last months he spent time working on the text that follows. He wanted it to be published, and we are grateful to Continuum for now putting it into print. Dilman was a prolific author and his readers already have many works by him on which to reflect. This final volume of his, however, very much deserves to see the light of day. Dilman was a scholar of international reputation. He specialized in moral philosophy and psychology, logic, and the philosophy of Wittgenstein. All of these interests of his surface in the present book.

Dilman was born in Turkey on 4 November 1930. Having gained a B.Sc. in chemistry from Robert College, Istanbul, he subsequently obtained a doctorate from Cambridge University under the direction of John Wisdom (1904–93). He took up a teaching position in the philosophy department at University College, Swansea, in 1961 and, apart from periods during which he worked at the University of California and the University of Hull, remained there until his retirement. He was awarded a personal chair at Swansea in 1984. He published 19 books and more than 70 articles. He was, indeed, a prolific writer.

Philosophy as Criticism allows us to read Dilman's reflections on a selection of texts by some very famous contemporary philosophers. Dilman is consistently critical of the works that he discusses, but he always takes pains to try to present what they say before commenting on them. As his colleague D. Z. Phillips said in an obituary, 'Dilman was a man of great integrity and loyalty, with a passion for truth and decency' (*Philosophical Investigations*, July 2003). Readers of *Philosophy as Criticism* will find that integrity and a passion for truth and decency abound in it.

As we have noted, the book was written while Ilham Dilman was dying. For reasons that one might guess, therefore, it needed a fair bit of editing, so as to be presented in a publishable form. We have tried to do our best to provide what we thought necessary, and hope that readers will find the result much worth reading.

Brian Davies and Mario von der Ruhr

Introduction

This manuscript did not start as a book; but if it becomes a book, it will be my last one. For I am terminally ill.

It started with the desire to read some well-known figures in philosophy which I had not read. In a way, I chose at random, except that I wanted my authors to be philosophers I would disagree with. And from each I chose a book. To people who asked, I said I was doing it for fun. This is perfectly true. The fun was in the challenge. But in a way, you could say it was masochistic fun. I wanted to be as fair to my chosen authors as possible. I can honestly say that I have no axe to grind. I wanted to be fair, and then to criticize.

Philosophy, in my understanding, is at least partly criticism. Where the disagreement is great, the criticism goes deep. Criticism: you could describe this as considering objections. This is what one does when, in philosophy, one follows one's own path, or opens up a new path.

One certainly learns from others in philosophy – in discussion with them, and in reading and considering what they have written. And if one is active and has an open mind, one continues to learn. But as one gets older, it is important to find one's own voice and one's own path.

What drove me to philosophy in my youth – my adolescence – were difficulties of life. I must, however, add that I have had a very lucky, wonderful childhood and youth. The difficulties were, I suppose, problems of growing up. These got me interested in Freud and in psycho-analysis. I studied philosophy in Cambridge in the early 1950s. I continued to be interested in philosophy, but with a tinge of disappointment. I had good tutors as an undergraduate. Dr Casimir Lewy stands out in my mind. He knew how to get the best from me, and he was very kind.

In my last years as an undergraduate, I read Professor John Wisdom's book *Philosophy and Psycho-Analysis*,[1] which had just been published. In my second and third terms, I went to his lectures, and they helped me discover in philosophy what I was seeking. Dr Lewy helped me to apply to do a Ph.D. in Cambridge. Professor Wisdom became my supervisor. I wrote a thesis entitled: *A Philosophical Investigation into Psycho-analysis*. After my first term, I moved to London to embark on personal analysis.

My way of working was totally unorthodox, and John Wisdom left me completely free to read what I wanted and do what I wished. I read very little philosophy, but a fair amount of psycho-analytic literature. I was like a bee who extracted most of my honey from the literature I read, the films I went to see, etc. I spent a year reading Proust's *À La Recherche du Temps Perdu*, which totally engrossed me and moved me.

There is no way I can describe the papers I wrote for John Wisdom. They were completely idiosyncratic. He always treated them with great seriousness and responded to them. At first, we had our supervisions in the waiting rooms at King's Cross or Liverpool Street Station. Then, he started seeing me at his sister's, who lived close to my own home. She was a wonderful person and took me under her wing. From time to time, John Wisdom and his wife Pamela would invite me to spend a weekend with them. I discussed philosophy with John, and went for walks with him. He sometimes invited a few other people from the faculty, such as Renford Bambrough and others. The idea was to give me the opportunity to discuss philosophy. But, as I remember, I was too shy and my contribution was negligible. Later, both John and Pamela separately met and stayed with my parents in Turkey. There was – I learned from my mother – instantaneous warmth and sympathy on both sides.

After I received my Ph.D. degree, I did my military service in Turkey for 18 months. At the end of it, I got married to my wife Anne. I had lost my father during the period of my military service. I knew that he wanted me to take up his business. This involved working in a starch/glucose factory, where he was one of the associates. The people there welcomed my proposal to do so. But I was not equipped for this. I tried it, without success, and gave it up after six months.

So, I sent letters of application for teaching jobs at British universities, without success. One evening, there was a cable from Rush Rhees, totally out of the blue. The philosophy department at Swansea University needed a tutor, and Professor Jones, the Head of Department, was away in America. I knew Rush Rhees only by name. He wanted to appoint a tutor without having to advertise it. So he got in touch with Dr Lewy and John Wisdom, and they both recommended me, partly to help me. The hope was that, once I had gained a foothold in the United Kingdom things would be much easier for me. I accepted the offer, and it opened up new horizons for me: first, the friendship with a wonderful person like Rush Rhees, and entry into a department in which I felt completely at home. I must also say that Rhees helped me in all sorts of ways, philosophically and otherwise. I felt so much at home in Swansea that I threw caution to the wind and never gave a thought to what I would do in the next academic year. Luck had it that the Swansea department upgraded the Tutorship to an Assistant Lectureship and appointed me to it.

I was away from Swansea for four years, one year in Santa Barbara, where I was offered an Assistant Professorship, then three years in Hull, where I was appointed Senior Lecturer. When there was an opportunity to return to Swansea, I took a demotion to Lecturer and then, very soon, was given a Readership. I must say that we had a lot of serious trouble in the department. We made light of the infighting and survived. I do not regret my return. I love Swansea, love walking on the Gower, which is a very beautiful place. And I consider the department my philosophical home.

A few words about my philosophical development. When I came to Swansea in 1961, the department was composed of Professor Jones, Rush Rhees, Roy Holland, and Peter Winch. I was their junior. They all gave me the hand of friendship. I considered myself very lucky. I attended Rush Rhees' lectures and seminars and also some of Peter Winch's. I learned a lot. I wrote two books, *Induction and Deduction: A study in Wittgenstein* and *Matter and Mind: Two Essays in Epistemology*.[2] There was nothing original in these books; they were my attempts to learn to understand Wittgenstein, and also to some extent John Wisdom and G. E. Moore. I also wrote a little book (with Dewi Phillips) on self-deception, *Sense and Delusion*.[3] It didn't do well, because it was off the beaten track. But I enjoyed writing it and debating it with Dewi.

I must say that, after this, I began to find my own voice slowly but surely. I have learned a very great deal from John Wisdom, Rush Rhees and Ludwig Wittgenstein, and to a lesser extent from Peter Winch and Roy Holland. But I do not think of myself as belonging to any school of thought. Whatever my contribution to philosophy may be, I believe it to be my own – though I repeat: with great indebtedness to my colleagues and teachers.

I am not an avid reader, and what's more, I am a slow reader. This book is not the result of a project, but simply the attempt to apply myself, at the end of my life, to a random collection of volumes. If I have made this introductory chapter somewhat autobiographical, it is to express the gratitude I feel for my life. I am sure that this gratitude makes it much easier to bear the separation from life that looms ahead of me.

Let me now turn more directly to philosophy. The topics of the books I chose to discuss at random – no premeditation was involved, and I came to them purely accidentally – are widely recognized topics in philosophy. But I did not find it easy to enter into these books, because their approach was, in so many ways, alien to me. If my life continues and these essays turn into a book, the unifying theme will be 'philosophy as criticism'.

In my understanding, philosophy begins with a problem. It proceeds with an attempt to understand the problem, to discover its roots and, as the discussion proceeds, to consider objections to the steps one takes. These steps, objectionable as they may be, may be forced on one. If one is to avoid them, one often needs to do a considerable amount of dismantling. It is also part of philosophical investigation to draw distinctions, especially between what is genuine and what is a false imitation, between what is merely appearance and what is reality, between what is shallow and what is deep. When one is considering another philosopher, one needs to consider objections to the steps he has taken. This is criticism. One also considers his approach: where has he come from, and where is he going? This may clash with one's own approach; but one must try not to be dismissive. One must try to be both honest and fair. This takes moral discipline.

Notes

1 John Wisdom, *Philosophy and Psycho-Analysis* (Oxford: Blackwell, 1953).
2 Ilham Dilman, *Induction and Deduction: A Study in Wittgenstein* (Oxford: Blackwell, 1973); *Matter and Mind: Two Essays in Epistemology* (London: Macmillan, 1975).
3 Ilham Dilman, *Sense and Delusion* (London: Routledge & Kegan Paul, 1971).

1 Dennett's Explanation of Consciousness

1. Dennett's Book *Consciousness Explained*

In the introductory chapter of the book, Section 4, Dennett says that he will 'attempt to explain consciousness': 'I will explain the various phenomena that compose what we call consciousness, showing how they are all physical effects of the brain's activities . . .'[1] By 'phenomena of consciousness' he means such things as 'seeing things' and 'feeling pain', including 'having hallucinations'. Thus, very briefly, when light from an object stimulates our optic nerve, the impulse along the nerve produces some electric activity in the brain, and it is this activity that makes us see – a causal account. If these particular nerves entering the brain could be stimulated artificially, we would see the same thing in the absence of the object seen. This would constitute an hallucination. Both would be the same phenomena of consciousness.

The suggestion is that brain activity produces or causes vision or pain in some ways like electricity attached to a bulb produces light – light rays or waves to be emitted – except for the fact that light waves are physical phenomena, like the flow of electrons that causes these. By contrast, the phenomena of consciousness are not physical phenomena like the electrical activity in the brain which Dennett claims are causing them. But, writes Dennett, 'the principle of the conservation of energy' is violated by such dualism. 'This confrontation between quite standard physics and dualism has been endlessly discussed since Descartes' own day, and is widely regarded as the inescapable and fatal flaw of dualism.'[2]

So, what does Dennett do? He reduces consciousness to brain activity – materialism. He admits that 'it is very hard to imagine how your mind could be your brain' but, he adds, 'not impossible'.[3] 'In order to imagine this, you really have to know a lot of what science has discovered about how brains work.'[4] Dennett goes on,

> but much more important, you have to learn new ways of thinking. Adding facts helps you imagine new possibilities, but the discoveries of neuroscience are not enough – even neuroscientists are often baffled by consciousness. In order to stretch your imagination, I will

provide, along with the relevant scientific facts, a series of stories, analogies, thought experiments, and other devices designed to give you new perspectives, break old habits of thought, and help you organize the facts into a single, coherent vision strikingly different from the traditional view of consciousness we tend to trust.[5]

Dennett points out, quite rightly, that again and again the progress of science involves conceptual innovations which wean us from what we have come to regard as obvious. However, if I may speak for myself, there is a difference between accepting a conceptual innovation and coming out of a conceptual confusion. Dennett rightly finds fault with Cartesian dualism and wishes to turn his back on it. However, he wrongly identifies it with what has come to be called 'folk psychology', and so finds fault with the everyday concepts in which we think of human life and behaviour, and wishes to replace them. In his commitment to find a scientific explanation of consciousness he shows little understanding of 'folk psychology', treating its concepts in a very cavalier fashion. What he needs is a *clarification* of the concept of consciousness, instead of an *explanation of it along scientific lines*.

Paradoxically, he has more in common with Cartesian metaphysics than folk psychology, which is in fact innocent of it. Thus, for instance, Descartes argued that he was a *res cogitans* – a thinking thing, a mind, and that he *had* a body which he could exist without. Similarly, on the materialistic side, Dennett finds nothing wrong with the idea that he is a brain and that, as such, he could exist in a vat without the rest of his body, while retaining his identity in the course of hallucinatory experiences, this body of his being a phantom body on the model of a phantom limb.

Let me put it this way. There is, of course, a science of neurophysiology, but you cannot get to an understanding of either consciousness or what makes a human being a human being from such a science, just as you cannot reach such an understanding if you start from a Cartesian mind identified as being separate from a flesh-and-blood human being. As Sartre puts it: 'Once the body has been separated from consciousness, no links will be able to rejoin it with consciousness'.[6] For such a separation turns it into a thing – and how can a thing *have* consciousness?[7] Once we separate the two, we are left with the idea of a person's body as a thing. It is not surprising that Dennett often refers to a human being as an 'entity' or a 'living body' – in other words, the body of physiology in function. That is *not* the human body which Wittgenstein referred to as 'the best picture of the human soul'.[8]

As for what Dennett refers to as 'the various phenomena that compose what we call consciousness' – a great motley which he lumps together, calling them 'states' and 'processes' – they are not something 'internal' or 'inner'. Consciousness is *originally* something external and as such 'visible to other people'. For its only expressions *in the first place* are the person's responses or reactions to what goes on around him. Only when the possibility of reflection brings these acts under his voluntary control does his consciousness – for instance his anger at having been insulted – acquire the possibility of existing apart from these acts, so that it can become something internal; that is, something he can keep to himself if he so chooses. I shall return to this in the last section of this chapter.

Dennett starts by emphasizing, again and again, the *mystery* of consciousness. This is the big *philosophical* puzzle or problem central to his book that he wishes to resolve.

What could be more obvious or certain to each of us than that he or she is a conscious subject or experience, an enjoyer of perceptions or sensations, a sufferer of pain, an entertainer of ideas, and a conscious deliberator? That seems undeniable, but what in the world can consciousness itself be? How can living physical bodies in the physical world produce such phenomena? That is the mystery.[9]

He continues:

My conscious thinking, and especially the enjoyment I felt in the combination of sunny light, sunny Vivaldi violins, rippling branches – plus the pleasure I took in just thinking about it all – how could *all that* be just something physical in my brain? How could any combination of electrochemical happenings in my brain somehow add up to the delightful way hundreds of twigs genuflected in time with the music? . . .[10]

Dennett is right, of course: 'How can living physical bodies [that is anatomical, physiological bodies] produce such phenomena?' They cannot. He considers 'the attractions of mind stuff': 'So we have discovered two sorts of things one might want to make out of mind stuff: the purple cow [the mental image] that isn't in the brain, and the thing that does the thinking. But there are still special powers we might want to attribute to mind stuff'.[11] He summarizes the 'four reasons for believing in mind stuff':

The conscious mind, it seems, cannot just *be* the brain . . . because nothing in the brain could

> be the medium in which the purple cow is rendered;
> be the thinking thing – the I;
> appreciate wine, . . . love someone . . .;
> act with moral responsibility.[12]

However, Dennett in the end goes along with science and its stuff, matter, its organization into structures, the functions they have within these organizations, and what these functions are capable of producing. He moves slowly, he doesn't jump, he tries to enlist the support of scientific work in neurophysiology:

> According to the various ideologies grouped under the label of *functionalism*, if you reproduced the *entire* 'functional structure' of the human wine taster's cognitive system . . ., you would thereby reproduce *all* the mental properties as well, including the enjoyment . . . If all the control functions of a human wine taster's brain can be reproduced in silicon chips, the enjoyment will *ipso facto* be reproduced as well.[13]

Dennett doesn't hurry: on the one hand, he doesn't make light of the difficulty he has been stressing all along, and on the other hand, he wishes to remain true to the scientific spirit of caution and thorough investigation and evidence:

> Some brand of functionalism may triumph in the end (in fact this book will defend a version of functionalism), but it seems outrageous at first blush. It seems that no mere machine, no matter how accurately it mimicked the brain processes of the human wine taster, would be capable of appreciating a wine, or a Beethoven sonata . . .[14]

Dennett thus finds himself between the devil and the deep blue sea.

> The idea of mind as distinct in this way from the brain, composed not of ordinary matter but of some other, special kind of stuff, is *dualism*, and it is deservedly in disrepute today . . . The prevailing wisdom . . . is *materialism*: there is only one sort of stuff, namely *matter* – the physical stuff of physics, chemistry, and physiology – and the mind is somehow nothing but a physical phenomenon. In short, the mind is the brain . . . It is one of the main burdens of this book to explain consciousness without ever giving in to the siren song of dualism.[15]

So, what is wrong with Cartesian dualism? How can two different substances interact?

> Since we don't have the faintest idea (yet) what properties mind stuff
> has, we can't even guess (yet) how it might be affected by physical
> processes emanating somehow from the brain, so let's ignore those
> upbound signals for the time being and concentrate on the return
> signals, the directives from mind to brain. These, ex hypothesi, are
> not physical; they are not light waves or sound waves or cosmic
> rays or streams of subatomic particles. No physical energy or mass
> is associated with them . . .[16]

This very idea of interaction contradicts 'the principle of the conservation
of energy . . .'[17] To put it in a language which even children would understand: 'How can Casper, the Friendly Ghost, glide through walls and grab
a falling towel? How can mind stuff both elude all physical measurement
and control the body?'[18] In short, it is 'this fundamentally antiscientific
stance of dualism' which for Dennett is 'its most disqualifying feature' and
the reason why he regards it as something 'to be avoided *at all costs* . . .
given the way dualism wallows in mystery, *accepting dualism is giving up*'.[19]

So, up to this point in the book, Dennett states his problem. He has to
turn away from dualism; but he is well aware of, and susceptible to, its
attraction: 'My conscious thinking . . . the enjoyment I felt . . . How could
all that be just something physical in my brain?'[20] And yet, on the other
side, how can two different substances interact? As I said, Dennett finds
himself between the devil and the deep blue sea. He opts for the path of
physical science and one-substance materialism, and gets to work. I hope
to consider, briefly, some of the steps he takes.

What I would like to point out at this stage is that Dennett's dilemma
has its source in seeing the problem in terms of a choice between stuffs or
substances – (1) substance, matter; or (2) matter and consciousness – consciousness conceived as an immaterial substance. He finds fault with the
everyday concepts in which we think of human life and behaviour, and
he wishes to replace them. He does not take this 'counter-intuitiveness'
sufficiently seriously, philosophically, and speaks of what is 'intuitively
obvious' here as 'spurious'. So, he leaves out an appreciation of the peculiar
logical dimension in which human existence has its characteristic identity,
the form of being which human beings have in the kind of life they live
in communities bound together with language and culture, their environment suffused with forms of significance which have their source in their
language and culture. He has a one-dimensional conception of reality.

Light and colour vision are produced by electro-magnetic rays. The chemical properties of different substances are explained in terms of their subatomic particles.

> Why should consciousness be the only thing that can't be explained [that way]? Solids and liquids and gases can be explained in terms of things that aren't themselves solids or liquids or gases. Surely life can be explained in terms of things that aren't themselves alive – and the explanation doesn't leave living things lifeless.[21]

Dennett shows no appreciation, for instance, that 'life' means different things. A plant, for example, is alive, but it does not have a life in the sense that a human being does. You can speak of the ingredients that have to come together, and the processes they have to sustain, for there to be a living plant. But human life is of an altogether different logical order. You cannot begin to understand it in these terms. Dennett often speaks in terms of a 'living human body' that is the body of anatomy, fulfilling its physiological functions. But this does not reveal the aspect under which a human being is a human being with a life – its joys and tribulations, feelings and concerns, thoughts and decisions that become for it possible objects of focus. What comes into focus with such a change in aspect is *a new dimension of reality*, in which human beings have their unique mode of existence or form of being. That is what we have to appreciate, and where we have to remain if we are to be clear about what consciousness is.

Of course, many animals are conscious beings, and they are conscious of different things, although the scope of their consciousnesses and the richness of its tapestry differ greatly and vary, within different degrees, from that which belongs to human life. All the same, it seems to me that we would appreciate best what consciousness amounts to, if we could keep our sight fixed on human life. To repeat: what we need for this purpose is a conceptual clarification, rather than a scientific explanation. That said, I now turn to some of the steps Dennett takes on the way to his thoroughly incoherent conclusion, where all his earlier caution is thrown to the wind.

2.   Steps Along the Way to Dennett's Conclusion

He begins semi-playfully with a light touch, considering a brain in a vat, kept alive, artificially stimulated, to make you hallucinate that you have a body when you don't, that you are sitting on a sandy beach, listening to music, and that you can wiggle the right index finger of your phantom body in the sand.[22] But, without a body, where are you? Right away, there is a problem which Dennett recognizes: Who is this 'you', this person, who is made to hallucinate? Presumably, he is the person whose brain has been kept alive in a vat, while the flesh-and-blood person himself is no longer in existence, the only body in existence being a phantom body – that is, an imaginary body, an hallucination. But again, whose hallucination? How can the brain be such a subject and/or intentional agent – a human subject and agent? And if not, how can it have experiences? From phantom limb to phantom body – that is a logical jump which it is impossible to make.

Only a person, a flesh-and-blood being, who has lived and shared a life with others, engaged with them, responded to his environment, and learned much in the course of such a life, including how to make sense of things, can have experiences in which he becomes conscious of what goes on in his surroundings. And unless he can apprehend things, he cannot *mis*apprehend them either; unless he is capable of being in touch with how things are, he cannot have hallucinations, either. In any case, hearing music is not a matter of having 'stereo music, suitably encoded as nerve impulses, piped into one's auditory nerves'.[23] Hearing music is not just having certain auditory sensations. One has to have lived and learned to hear and enjoy music. You can produce electrical impulses in a brain kept alive in a vat; but who is supposed to be listening to and hearing music? An hallucinating person in a phantom body? We have lapsed into total incoherence. In any case, Dennett reassures us: 'We are not brains in vats – in case you were worried'.[24]

Next, Dennett is prepared to take his first serious step: 'If dualism is the best we can do, we can't understand human consciousness'.[25] He continues: 'Some people are convinced that we can't in any case'.[26] But such 'defeatism, today, in the midst of a cornucopia of scientific advances ready to be exploited' strikes Dennett as 'ludicrous, even pathetic'.[27] 'Dualism [is] the idea that a brain cannot be a thinking thing so a thinking thing cannot be a brain... Adopting dualism is really just accepting defeat without admitting it.'[28] True, 'adopting materialism does not by itself dissolve the puzzles about consciousness'.[29] Dennett looks forward: 'Somehow the brain must be the mind, but unless we come to see in some detail how this is possible, our materialism will not explain consciousness ...'[30] However, Dennett warns us that his theory seems to be strongly at odds with common wisdom, and that we should not, therefore, expect it to make comfortable reading.

So, in the next two chapters – 3 and 4 – Dennett examines what constitutes our consciousness and how it can be identified with goings-on in the brain. He refers to the former as 'the fauna and flora ... that inhabit conscious experience',[31] 'the things that swim in the stream of consciousness',[32] 'all the wonderful things that inhabit other people's minds', 'materials of our inner lives', 'the intervening variable between external stimulus and behavioural response', 'denizens of the phenomenological garden'.[33] He restates the principal difficulty that he has to resolve: 'How could anything composed of material particles *be* the fun that I'm having? . . . Finding a materialistic account that does justice to all these phenomena will not be easy'.[34]

Dennett makes a valiant, imaginative effort. For him, though, Cartesian dualism 'and scientific materialism' stand in stark contrast to each other with no alternative third perspective. Something of the Cartesian conception of the inner world of consciousness, divorced from our so-called outer life lived in the arena of our engagements, clings to him. In the end, despite all his efforts, Dennett's decision to leave the identification of the contents of consciousness with events and states in the brain to empirical investigation, is abrupt and stretches credulity.

Let me consider briefly the rather tortuous path he follows to this conclusion. Dennett's Cartesian heritage is the logical, conceptual divorce he accepts between the inner and the outer, between consciousness and human life in the arena of engagement and interaction, between body and soul in the flesh-and-blood human being. He keeps asking: what makes you think that these so-called animals are *animals* and not just fur-covered robots?[35] 'Now, some of these adult human beings *may* be zombies',[36] for 'you can't tell a zombie from a normal person by examining external behaviour. Since that is all we ever get to see of our friends and neighbours, *some of your best friends may be zombies*'.[37] And again:

> The fact that *there is* a single, coherent interpretation of a sequence of behaviour doesn't establish that the interpretation is *true*; it might be only *as if* the 'subject' were conscious; we risk being taken in by a zombie with no inner life at all.[38]

This is the old philosophical problem of 'other minds' in a modern setting. So, Dennett develops, as he puts it, 'a neutral method for investigating and describing phenomenology'.[39] He calls it 'heterophenomenology'. It follows a 'mental path' and insists on 'the third-person point of view'.[40] Dennett compares this task to the task of the reader of a novel in interpreting the novel – a work of fiction. What the reader is concerned with here, is to make sense of the story. The question is not, 'Is the story true?', but 'What does it add up to? What sense does it make?'

So, what the heterophenomenologist is interested in, is not what actually takes place in the other person's consciousness, in his thoughts and feelings. For this, Dennett holds, is something we cannot know: 'We can't be sure that the speech acts we observe express real beliefs about actual experiences'.[41] What the reader of the novel does, is to let the text '*constitute* a (fictional) world, a world determined by fiat by the text'[42] – that is, one constructed by the author, the novelist. This gives the character in the novel a life that makes sense. Similarly, Dennett says, 'the heterophenomenologist lets the subject's text *constitute* that subject's *heterophenomenological world* . . .'.[43] He adds a bit further down that the world of the subject, thus constructed, 'will be a stable, intersubjectively confirmable theoretical posit, having the same metaphysical status as, say, Sherlock Holmes' London . . .'[44]

Dennett compares this way of making sense of a person's behaviour and experiences with the way an anthropologist can make sense of the life of an alien people. He is not interested in the question of the truth, the literal truth, of their beliefs, but in the role they play in the life they live, the way they transform that life, give it the dimensions of meaning which characterize it.

So, this is relevant to understanding a person. But it leaves the question, 'What is consciousness?' untouched, sealed within a person's 'inner world', cut off from his so-called 'outer life' and behaviour. Part of the reason for this result is the way Dennett conceives of consciousness as made up of some special stuff – the raw materials of our inner lives, the phenomena visible only to one person in inner vision. Quite a bit of heavy weather follows, and then, without any real argument, the predestined conclusion is adopted:

> My suggestion, then, is that if we were to find real goings-on in people's brains that had enough of the 'defining' properties of the items that populate their heterophenomenological worlds, we could reasonably propose that we had discovered what they were *really* talking about – even if they initially resisted the identifications. And if we discovered that the real goings-on bore only a minor resemblance to the heterophenomenological items, we could reasonably declare that people were just mistaken in the beliefs they expressed, in spite of their sincerity . . .[45]

Even then, Dennett still repeats in the very next paragraph: 'Brain events seem too different from phenomenological items to be the real referents of the beliefs we express in our introspective reports'.[46] So, he proposes 'to stretch our imagination some more', to make the identification more imaginable.

3. Dennett's Philosophical Problems with Consciousness

Dennett expresses the problem he finds with consciousness in terms of the difference, if there is any, between an ordinary person and a zombie. 'Philosophers' zombies', he writes, 'are not really conscious at all, in spite of the fact that they are, at their best, behaviourally indistinguishable from a conscious person.'[47] Hence, our best friend may, in fact, be a zombie. That is, Dennett starts by saying that there is a difference between persons and zombies, and that this difference is the presence of consciousness in the former and its absence in the latter, but that this difference is totally undetectable from the outside. Zombies 'may have internal states with functional content . . . but these are unconscious [i.e. neural] states that merely cause [them] to go into some further unconscious [neural] state that directs the process of generating and executing a so-called speech act composed of "canned" formulae'.[48] Dennett then introduces the concept of a zimbo. 'A zimbo is a zombie that, as a result of self-monitoring, has internal (but unconscious) higher order informational states that are about its other, lower-order informational states . . . A zimbo is just a zombie that is behaviourally complex, thanks to a control system that permits recursive self-representation.'[49]

He notes a bit further on that he offers 'this parable of the zimbos tongue in cheek, since I don't think either the concept of a zombie or the folk-psychological categories of higher-order thoughts can survive except as relics of a creed outworn'.[50] Reverting to Cartesian dualism, he writes: 'Witnesses [Descartes' thinking thing, the inner observer] need raw materials on which to base their judgements. These raw materials, whether they are called "sense data" or "sensations" or "raw feels" or "phenomenal properties of experience", are props with which a witness makes no sense'.[51] But they are held in place by various illusions supported by 'a nearly impenetrable barrier of intuitions. The task of this chapter is to break through that barrier'.[52]

On the one hand, Dennett wants to take a proper perspective on what he regards as the contents of 'the phenomenological garden'; on the other hand, he looks for 'evidence about how the mind is accomplished by the brain'.[53] He discusses the example of 'blind-sight', which he characterizes as a 'partial zombiehood'. Dennett asks what is going on here. Is this 'visual perception without consciousness – of the sort that a mere automaton might exhibit?'[54] He gives examples where different forms of 'behaviour' are controlled 'without any help from consciousness' – that is, automatically.[55]

What about the contents of consciousness as conceived by philosophers – 'raw feels', 'sense', 'intrinsic properties of conscious experiences', 'the qualitative content of mental states', or 'qualia'? Dennett says: 'There are subtle differences in how these terms have been defined, but I'm going to ride roughshod over them ... I *am* denying that there are any such properties. But ... I agree wholeheartedly that there seem to be qualia'.[56] Again: 'The sort of difference that people imagine there to be between any machine and any human experience ... is one I am firmly denying: there is no such sort of difference. There just seems to be'.[57]

Towards the end of the chapter entitled 'Qualia Disqualified', Dennett wonders how on earth 'all this could indeed be just a combination of electrochemical happenings in my brain ... it doesn't seem to be.' He responds: 'Haven't we given ourselves grounds for concluding that with a brain organized the way ours is, this is just the sort of heterophenom-enological world we would expect? Why shouldn't such combinations of electrochemical happenings in the brain have precisely the effects we set out to explain?'[58]

If consciousness is a kind of private shadow-show or collection of hal-lucinatory images, then indeed why not? As I said at the outset of this chapter, it is like explaining the lighting of a bulb by means of an electric current entering the filament. Consciousness, however, is not some special inner light. Dennett goes on in the same way in the next chapter:

> How could a complicated slew of information-processing events in a bunch of silicon chips amount to conscious experiences? But it's just as difficult to imagine how an organic human brain could support consciousness. How could a complicated slew of electromagnetic interactions between billions of neurons amount to conscious experi-ence? And yet we readily imagine human beings to be conscious, even if we still can't imagine how this could be.[59]

And a bit further down:

> The 'software' or 'virtual machine' level of description I have exploited in this book is exactly the sort of mediating level [Colin] McGinn describes: not explicitly physiological or mechanical and yet capable of providing the necessary bridges to the brain machinery on the one hand, while on the other hand not being explicitly phe-nomenological and yet capable of providing the necessary bridges to the world of content, the world of heterophenomenology. We've done it! We have imagined how a brain could produce conscious experience ...[60]

I am afraid I do not see that we have. Dennett had set his sights on arriving at a materialistic theory of consciousness. He has come to it by hook or by crook. Consciousness is not and cannot be the product of brain activity – even though, it is true, there cannot be consciousness without the complex electrical activities in the brain studied by neuroscientists. I shall try to explain all this in the final section of this chapter.

Before doing so, I want to quote a few more sentences whose reassurances of the direction in which Dennett has moved strike me as totally empty:

> McGinn just notes that it seems obvious to him that there is nothing to be hoped for from this quarter. This spurious 'obviousness' is a great obstacle to progress in understanding consciousness ... This seems obvious until you look quite hard at what we might learn about the brain's activities, and begin trying to imagine, in detail, an alternative model. Then what happens is rather like the effect of learning how a stage magician performs a conjuring trick. Once we take a serious look backstage, we discover that we didn't actually see what we thought we saw on stage. The huge gap between phenomenology and physiology shrinks a bit; we see that some of the 'obvious' features of phenomenology are not real at all . . .[61]

I am not concerned to defend phenomenology, but I do not see how learning more about the brain's activity is going to help with the problem of understanding consciousness. The problem is a *conceptual* one and calls for a different kind of work altogether.

4.   An Alternative Approach: What is Consciousness?

Wittgenstein writes: 'Only of a living human being and what resembles (behaves like) a living human being can one say: it has sensations; it sees; is blind; hears; is deaf; is conscious or unconscious'.[62] 'He is conscious' denies, for instance, that he is in a coma, unconscious. But if he is unconscious, then he is alive and hopefully has a chance of recovering, of regaining consciousness. Furthermore, whether he is conscious or not is clearly open to view. It is the person, the flesh-and-blood being, who is said to be conscious, and this cuts across the Cartesian dichotomy of body and soul – the anatomical body and what Descartes regarded as the immaterial soul, aware of itself and hidden from others.

Second, a person may be conscious of many different things. He may have a headache, for example, or he may have been unfairly stopped from expressing an objection and left with a feeling of resentment. We refer to these as 'the contents of his consciousness'. There need be nothing hidden about these, either; his feeling of resentment, for instance, unless of course the person positively hides it from others. Such contents of his conscious-ness are not some special stuff, 'patches of oil in a spiritual substance', as John Wisdom once put it. They are forms of awareness in the person's responses to what concerns him in situations that face him in his life. The responses are expressions of his awareness in those situations of what he is faced with, of what matters to him, of what exercises him. For anybody who belongs to that life, who engages with it and shares it, there is nothing hidden about what is at stake for the person in his responses, about what it is he is responding to. He can, of course, conceal it from others, not let it appear in his responses, or pretend that things are otherwise.

Put it like this: what he feels or responds to in his feelings, what he makes affective contact with, has two aspects: an outer aspect, to which he gives expression in his language, behaviour and bodily demeanour, including facial expressions where others can *see* it, and an inner aspect of what remains of it in his feelings when he checks or suppresses what would otherwise be visible to others. What can thus be seen by others when he has no reason to hide it and so does not conceal it, *and* what continues to exercise him in his feelings, are parts of the same thing. We could say, therefore, that there is nothing necessarily hidden about the so-called inner life. The idea of an inner life made up of some special stuff – the phenomenological garden – is a philosopher's myth, a symptom of conceptual confusion.

Let me briefly quote from Chapter 4 ('The Inner and the Outer in Human Life') of my book *Love and Human Separateness*[63]:

The child does not learn to express his feelings. For his feelings do not, in the first place, exist in separation from his responses. What he learns is to give *verbal* expression to them. This is not learning to describe them, nor is it learning to describe something that goes on within his consciousness. For we have seen that the feelings in ques-tion do not lie within him, but in his reactions, where others can see them. What he learns is a new way of expressing them, these new expressions becoming the object of appropriate responses from his parents and others around him. In many cases they take the place of the natural, primitive reactions, and since the utterance of verbal expressions is something he can do at will (for it is something he learns to do) it brings the expression of his feelings under his vol-untary control. Now it becomes possible for the child who wants to elicit certain responses from his parents to say that he is angry or distressed when he is not, even to pretend. He can also control his anger, check its expression, restrain his impulse to shout. Concealing one's anger is thus logically a more sophisticated form of behaviour than giving vent to it or displaying it . . . In this account the Cartesian view is reversed. A feeling, for instance, is not, in the first place, an inner thing which we then learn to describe. The person who has the feeling has, of course, a unique relation to it, in the sense that it is *his* – the man who shouts in anger is him, the mouth out of which the shout comes is his mouth, the fists that are clenched are his fists and it is he who clenches them. Nevertheless, originally, it is something which lies open to view where others can see it. What we learn early in life is to give verbal expression in what lies in our natural reactions. Thus originally our feelings are not hidden; being hidden is not their natural state. On the contrary we learn to hide our feelings, to contain our emotions, to suppress our natural reactions.[64]

I shall quote a little more:

As [Stuart] Hampshire puts it: the expression of an emotion is not 'something that may or may not be added to the emotion – as it would be if it were a mere description of something that has an existence independent of it . . . The truth is the reverse of this: 'the natural expression [of an emotion] is originally constitutive of the emotion itself and may or may not [later] be subtracted from it.' Thus the retaliatory reaction in the case of anger is an integral part of what we *understand* by 'anger'; it is internal to our *concept* of anger. Any explanation of the meaning of the word would thus have to contain some reference to such behaviour, as well as to the significance attributed by the subject to that which such behaviour is a response. But, of course, this does not mean that in a particular case one cannot have the emotion without exhibiting the behavioural response. When the behaviour is checked, the physiognomy with which it belongs is suppressed, then the emotion exists hidden from others. It remains alive though in the person's thoughts, in the inclination which he checks and in his changed bodily rhythm.[65]

So, one point is that consciousness and its contents are not hidden in the first place; nor are they intrinsically hidden from others. It is we who hide them from others when we have learned to do so. Secondly, the real dichotomy is not between body and mind, or body and soul. The real dichotomy is between human life, the kind of life in which human beings have their characteristic existence and mode of being, on the one hand, and material or physical existence and its diverse phenomena, on the other. Dennett seems to be almost wholly oblivious of human life and the form of being or existence that it makes possible. Of course we are flesh-and-blood beings and physical existence does encroach into our lives. When all is well and our bodies function properly, this functioning is invisible and unintrusive. It is only when something goes wrong that the physical makes its appearance in our lives. We want to move our limbs, for example, but fail to do so; or our bodies become a burden.

Physical science, in the form of medicine, can then come to our aid and, if we are lucky, put right what has gone wrong. We can then once more exercise our agency as intentional beings. We pick up our lives and try to live them in accordance with our lights, negotiating our share of obstacles and difficulties with which life presents us. As human beings, we have various resources and capacities to help us make our way.

Our mind is not some special immaterial substance. No, it is a complex of interdependent capacities that we have as flesh-and-blood beings in a life of speech and language that we share with others like ourselves, participating in common pursuits and practices, engaging with situations of such a shared life, suffused with the forms of significance that come from the life of our language. Here we are in an entirely different logical space from the one in which Dennett searches for our existence as human beings, viz. in the workings of our brains. I do not see that it requires much thought to see that what makes us human beings cannot possibly appear in the workings of our brains.

The last paragraph of Dennett's book reads: 'Several philosophers have seen what I am doing as a kind of redoing of Wittgenstein's attack on the "objects" of conscious experience. Indeed it is'.[66] All I can say is that Dennett and his philosophical allies must be living on a different planet.

Notes

1 Daniel Dennett, *Consciousness Explained* (London: Penguin, 1991), 16.
2 Ibid., 35.
3 Ibid.
4 Ibid.
5 Ibid., 16–17.
6 Jean-Paul Sartre, *L'Être et le néant* (Paris: Gallimard, 1943), 368. My translation.
7 Ludwig Wittgenstein, *Philosophical Investigations*, trans. G. E. M. Anscombe (Oxford: Blackwell, 1999), §283.
8 Ludwig Wittgenstein, *Culture and Value*, 2nd Revised Edition, ed. G. H. von Wight, trans. Peter Winch (Oxford: Blackwell, 1998), 56.

 9 Dennett, *Consciousness Explained*, 25.
10 Ibid., 26–7.
11 Ibid., 30.
12 Ibid., 33.
13 Ibid., 31.
14 Ibid.
15 Ibid., 33.
16 Ibid., 34.
17 Ibid., 35.
18 Ibid.
19 Ibid., 37.
20 Ibid., 26.
21 Ibid., 455.
22 Ibid., 5.
23 Ibid., 4.
24 Ibid., 7.
25 Ibid., 39.
26 Ibid., 40.
27 Ibid.
28 Ibid., 41.
29 Ibid.
30 Ibid., 41–2.
31 Ibid., 44.
32 Ibid., 45.
33 Ibid., 65.
34 Ibid., 65.
35 Ibid., 43.
36 Ibid., 72.
37 Ibid., 73.
38 Ibid., 78.
39 Ibid., 98.
40 Ibid., 72.
41 Ibid., 78.
42 Ibid., 81.
43 Ibid.
44 Ibid.
45 Ibid., 85.
46 Ibid.
47 Ibid., 309.
48 Ibid.
49 Ibid., 310.

50 Ibid., 313–14.
51 Ibid., 322.
52 Ibid.
53 Ibid., 322.
54 Ibid., 325.
55 Ibid., 329.
56 Ibid., 372.
57 Ibid., 375.
58 Ibid., 410.
59 Ibid., 433.
60 Ibid., 434.
61 Ibid.
62 Ludwig Wittgenstein, *Philosophical Investigations*, §281.
63 Ilham Dilman, *Love and Human Separateness* (Oxford: Blackwell, 1987).
64 Ibid., 50.
65 Ibid., 52–3.
66 Dennett, *Consciousness Explained*, 462.

2 John Searle's Defence of Realism

I

In the Introduction to his book *The Construction of Social Reality*, John Searle argues that 'we live in exactly one world' and that 'the most fundamental features of that world are as described by physics, chemistry, and the other natural sciences'.[1] But this world, Searle continues, contains 'phenomena that are not in any obvious way physical or chemical', and this 'gives rise to puzzlement': 'How, for example, can there be states of consciousness or meaningful speech acts as parts of the physical world?'[2] Searle writes:

> Many of the philosophical problems that most interest me have to do with how the various parts of the world relate to each other – how does it all hang together? . . . How do we get from the physics of utterances to meaningful speech acts performed by speakers and writers? . . . How does a mental reality, a world of consciousness, intentionality, and other mental phenomena, fit into a world consisting entirely of physical particles in fields of force?[3]

He adds:

> This book extends the investigation to social reality: How can there be an objective world of money, property, marriage, governments, elections, football games, cocktail parties and law courts in a world that consists entirely of physical particles, in fields of force, and in which some of these particles are organised into systems that are conscious biological beasts, such as ourselves?[4]

With regard to 'social reality', Searle says, 'the main question is, How do we construct an objective social reality?'[5] He writes: 'In early drafts of the book I devoted an initial chapter to defending realism, the idea that there is a real world independent of our thought and talk . . . I think that realism and a correspondence conception [of truth] are essential presuppositions of any sane philosophy, not to mention of any science . . .'[6] In the final version of his book, the discussion and defence of realism occupy

Chapters 7 and 8; the correspondence conception of truth is discussed in Chapter 9.

Early in Chapter 1, Searle distinguishes between and contrasts what he calls 'institutional facts', which depend on human agreement, with what he calls 'brute facts'. He also argues that, if there are to be any institutional facts, there must be brute facts which are entirely independent of human institutions and human agreement. He gives an example: 'In order that this piece of paper should be a five dollar bill, there has to be the human institution of money'.[7] But that this dollar bill is a piece of paper is independent of any human institution.

'Many people', he writes, 'including even a few whose opinions I respect, have argued that all of reality is somehow a human creation, that there are no brute facts, but only facts dependent on the human mind.' He adds: 'I want to defend the contrast . . . I want to defend the idea that there is a reality that is totally independent of us'.[8] Thus, later on in the book he speaks of 'the logical priority of brute facts over institutional facts':

> The structure of institutional facts is the structure of hierarchies of the form 'X counts as Y in context C'. That hierarchy has to bottom out in phenomena whose existence is not a matter of human agreement . . . As I said, earlier, all sorts of things can be money, but there has to be some physical realization, some brute fact – even if it is a bit of paper or a blip on a computer disk – on which we can impose our institutional form of status function. Thus there are no institutional facts without brute facts.[9]

But let us return to Chapter 1 of Searle's book. In a short section entitled 'Fundamental Ontology', he writes that

> two features of our conception of reality are not up for grabs. They are not . . . optional for us as citizens of the late twentieth and early twenty-first century. It is a condition of your being an educated person in our era that you are apprised of these two theories: the atomic theory of matter and the evolutionary theory of biology.[10]

Searle continues:

> Types of living systems evolve through natural selection, and some of them have evolved certain sorts of cellular structures, specifically nervous systems capable of causing and sustaining consciousness. Consciousness is a biological, and therefore physical, though of

course also mental, feature of certain higher-level nervous systems, such as human brains and a large number of different types of animal brains . . . With consciousness comes intentionality, the capacity of the mind to represent objects and states of affairs in the world other than itself.[11]

The section concludes as follows:

Here, then, are the bare bones of an ontology: We live in a world made up entirely of physical particles in fields of force. Some of these are organised into systems. Some of these systems are living systems and some of these living systems have evolved consciousness.[12]

Here then we are given, at one go, 'the condition of our being an educated person in our [present] era' and the 'fundamental ontology' that Searle takes any enlightened philosopher to be committed to.

Thus, the fundamental ontology in question, the one which consists of 'brute facts' which exist independently of us, consists of 'physical systems'. By contrast with this ontology, we have 'social reality' and also 'mental reality'. But *The Construction of Social Reality* concentrates mainly on 'social reality'. In Chapter 3, Searle argues that 'language is essentially constitutive of institutional reality'.[13] Consistent with what has gone on earlier in the book, Searle distinguishes between *language-independent facts* and facts that are *language-dependent*, and similarly between *language-independent thoughts* and *language-dependent* ones.[14] That Mount Everest has snow and ice at the summit is, he says, a language-independent fact. As he puts it: 'Take away all language and Mount Everest still has snow and ice near the summit'.[15] By contrast, 'facts about money and property (though they do not on the surface appear to be language dependent) are in fact language dependent'.[16]

Searle gives the following example of a language-dependent thought: 'A touchdown (in a game of football) counts for six points'.[17] He writes:

There are no prelinguistic perceptions of points, nor prelinguistic beliefs about points, because there is nothing there to perceive or have beliefs about except the relevant symbolic devices. The animal cannot prelinguistically see points the way it can see the cat up the tree, nor can it prelinguistically desire points the way it desires food.[18]

A bit further along, we read:

Even if we don't have words for 'man', 'line', 'ball', etc., we can see the man cross that line carrying that ball, and thus we can think a thought without words, which thought we would report in the words 'The man crossed the line carrying the ball'. But we cannot in addition see the man score six points because there is nothing in addition to see. The expression 'six points' does not refer to some language-independent objects in the way that the expression 'the man', 'the ball', 'the line' and 'the Evening Star' refer to language-independent objects. Points are not 'out there' in the way that planets, men, balls, and lines are out there.[19]

He continues:

Without language we can see the man cross a white line holding a ball, and without language we can want a man to cross a white line holding a ball. But we cannot see the man score six points or want the man to score six points without language, because points are not something that can be thought of or that can exist independently of words or other sorts of markers. And what is true of points in games is true of money, government, private property, etc., as we will see.[20]

Searle then moves on to a consideration of what he calls 'institutional facts'. These, he says, 'exist only by way of collective agreement, and there can be no prelinguistic way of formulating the content of the agreement, because there is no prelinguistic natural phenomena there'.[21] Let me mention just two of his examples – the first one in his own words:

Suppose I train my dog to chase dollar bills and bring them back to me in return for food. He still is not buying the food and the bills are not money to him. Why not? Because he cannot represent to himself the relevant deontic phenomena. He might be able to think 'If I give him this he will give me that food'. But he cannot think, for example, now I have the *right to buy* things, and when someone else has this he will also have the right to buy things.[22]

The other example involves a range of mountains which constitute the frontier between two countries.[23] Searle speaks of the mountains as natural objects and of their existence as a 'brute fact'. But to regard the range as a frontier presupposes the acceptance of certain legal agreements, which in turn presupposes the kind of life we live with language. I have put this in my own way, and shall return to it later. As Searle puts it: 'The mountains now symbolize something beyond themselves; they function like words'.[24] He goes on: 'Physically X – the range of the mountains – and Y – the frontier – are exactly the same thing. The only difference is that we have imposed a status on the X element, and this new status needs *markers*, because, empirically speaking, there isn't anything else there'.[25] Searle then summarizes his position as follows:

> Because the Y level of the shift from X to Y in the creation of institutional facts has no existence apart from its representation, we need some way of representing it. But there is no natural prelinguistic way to represent it, because the Y element has no natural prelinguistic features in addition to the X element that would provide the means of representation.[26]

Again as he puts it:

> The move from the brute to the institutional status is *eo ipso* a linguistic move, because the X term now symbolizes something beyond itself. But that symbolic move requires thoughts. In order to think the thought that constitutes the move from the X term to the Y status, there must be a vehicle of thought. You have to have something to think with. The physical features of the X term are insufficient for the content of the thought, but any object whatever that can be conventionally used and thought of as the bearer of that content can be used to think the thought. The last objects to think with are words, because that is part of what words are for.[27]

To highlight what lies at the centre of his argument, Searle says that when we move from X to Y, we 'attach a sense, a symbolic function, to an object that does not have that sense intrinsically . . . [to objects that] do not stand for something beyond themselves'.[28] As I understand it, Searle's view is that a stone is a stone, a mountain is a mountain, irrespective of the language in which we name these objects; but this is not true of a frontier or a dollar bill. As he puts it:

> Symbols do not create cats and dogs and evening stars; they create only the possibility of referring to cats and dogs and evening stars in a publicly accessible way. But symbolization creates the very ontological categories of money, property, points scored in games and political offices, as well as the categories of words, and speech acts.[29]

Apart from 'physicalism', this distinction lies at the heart of Searle's 'real-ism'. I therefore want to turn to the two chapters in which he considers and defends realism, viz. Chapters 7 and 8 ('Does the Real World Exist?'). Here, he says: 'The whole analysis presupposes a distinction between facts dependent on us and those that exist independently of us'[30] – that is, between 'social and institutional facts' and 'brute facts'. Searle continues: 'It is now time to defend the contrast on which the analysis rests, to defend the idea that there is a reality totally independent of us'.[31] He defines realism as 'the view that the world exists independently of our representations of it' and argues that 'Mount Everest exists independently of how or whether I or anyone else ever represented it or anything else'.[32] In the first of the two chapters he considers 'the argument from conceptual relativity against realism'. The idea of conceptual relativity, he says, is 'correct': 'Any system of classification or individuation, indeed, any system of representation at all is conventional, and to that extent arbitrary. The world divides up the way we divide it.'[33] By 'arbitrary', I think, he simply means 'human' – in other words: a system of representation is not prescribed or dictated by something that exists independently of us – i.e., we have a choice. If I may make up an example, we can classify the tomatoes we are going to sell in our greengrocer's shop according to their weight, or their size, or the darkness of their colour. We may even assign them a name as well as a price. But (I take it that this is Searle's argument or defence) which basket they appear in, makes no difference to the tomatoes found in the shop. It is because of what exists independently of our classification that we classify one way or another. Let me quote Searle again:

> ER1 [External Realism]: Reality exists independently of our representations of it.
>
> CR 1 [Conceptual Relativism]: All representations of reality are made relative to some more or less arbitrary selected set of concepts.
>
> So stated, these two views do not even have the *appearance* of inconsistency. The first just says that there is something out there to be described. The second says that we have to select a set of concepts and a vocabulary to describe it.[34]

Searle briefly considers different ways of making a map of a particular corner of the world – the North of India. 'Next', he says, imagine that eventually the humans all cease to exist. Now what happens to the existence of the Himalayas and all the facts about the Himalayas in the course of these vicissitudes? Absolutely nothing. Different descriptions of facts, objects, etc., came and went, but the facts, objects, etc., remained unaffected. (Does anyone really doubt this?)[35]

Searle continues: 'The fact that alternative conceptual schemes allow for different descriptions of the same reality, and that there are no descriptions of reality outside all conceptual schemes, has no bearing whatever on the truth of realism.'[36] He adds that conceptual relativity presupposes realism 'because it presupposes a language-independent reality that can be carved up or divided up in different ways, by different vocabularies'.[37] Let me give one more quotation:

> That we use the word 'cat' the way we do is up to us; that there is an object that exists independently of that use, and satisfies that use, is a plain matter of (absolute, intrinsic, mind-independent) fact. Contrary to Goodman, we do not make 'worlds'; we make *descriptions* that the actual world may fit or fail to fit. But all this implies that there is a reality that exists independently of our system of concepts. Without such a reality, there is nothing to apply the concept to.[38]

At the end of the chapter, Searle provides a partial diagnosis of why so many competent philosophers attack realism:

> One of the oldest usages in Western philosophy is to think that somehow or other truth and reality should coincide . . . [that] truth would have to provide an exact mirror of reality . . . When the philosopher despairs of achieving an exact isomorphism between the structure of reality and the structure of true representations, the temptation is to think that somehow or other our naïve notions of truth and reality have been discredited. But they have not been discredited. What has been discredited is a certain misconception of the relationship between truth and reality.[39]

Searle explains that 'it is only from a point of view that we represent reality, [whereas] ontologically objective reality does not have a point of view'.[40] So many philosophers conclude that our various representations of reality are all that we have, and that there is no such thing as 'ontologically objective reality'. In the second of the chapters concerned with realism ('Does the Real World Exist?')[41] Searle asks whether there are any arguments in favour of realism. He begins by mentioning Kant's thought that 'it is a scandal to philosophy that there has not been a proof of the [so called] external world', and Moore's attempt to provide such a proof by holding up his two hands. Searle says that 'we need to explain both our urge to prove external realism and our sense that any proof begs the question'.[42]

Searle rightly distinguishes between trying to show that this or that claim 'corresponds or fails to correspond to how things really are in the "external world"', and trying to show 'that the claim that there is an external world corresponds to how things are in the external world'.[43] The latter claim is not an empirical claim, thesis or hypothesis; it is 'the condition of having certain sorts of theses or hypotheses'. 'External Realism', that is the claim that there is an external world independently of us, 'is a purely formal [claim], without any specific content', and the only argument there can be for it would be a 'transcendental' argument.[44] 'The point we are attempting to show is that for a large class [of utterances] a condition of intelligibility for the normal understanding of those utterances is that there is a way things are that is independent of human representations'.[45] In other words, when we make such claims, enunciate such utterances, we 'presuppose external realism'.[46] But there can be no proof or argument for external realism that is not question-begging:[47]

> A public language presupposes a public world in the sense that many (not all) utterances of a public language purport to make references to phenomena that are ontologically objective, and they ascribe such-and-such features to these phenomena . . . [T]hat requirement is precisely the requirement of external realism. And the consequence of this point for the present discussion is that efforts to communicate in a public language require that we presuppose a public world. And the sense of "public" in question requires that the public reality exists independently of *representations* of that reality . . . The point is simply that when we understand an utterance [such as Mount Everest has snow and ice near the summit] we understand it as presupposing a publicly accessible reality.[48]

In the penultimate section of the chapter Searle rightly points out that 'there is still an ambiguity' in what he has argued so far:[49]

> Talk of money and marriages is talk of a publicly accessible reality, and such phenomena are 'representation independent' in the sense that this twenty dollar bill or this marriage between Sam and Sally exist independently of your or my representations of it.[50]

So what is the difference between them? Searle's answer is that 'marriages and money, unlike mountains and atoms, do not exist independently of all representations'.[51] This is how he elucidates the claim:

> [A] socially constructed reality presupposes a reality independent of all social constructions, because there has to be something for the construction to be constructed out of. To construct money, property, and language, for example, there have to be the raw materials of bits of metal, paper, land, sounds, and marks, for example. And the raw materials cannot in turn be socially constructed without presupposing some even rawer materials out of which they are constructed, until eventually we reach a bedrock of brute physical phenomena independent of all representations.[52]

Searle continues: 'To the "transcendental argument" of the previous section – a public language presupposes a public world – we add a "transcendental argument" in this section – a socially constructed reality presupposes a nonsocially constructed reality'.[53] He repeats: 'It is a logical consequence of the main argument of the book that you cannot have institutional facts without brute facts'.[54] Either way, 'our ordinary linguistic practices presuppose external realism'. There is a reality totally independent of us.[55]

II

I have tried to give a fair account of Searle's 'external realism' and of what he calls 'the construction of social reality'. I would now like to consider his physicalism and his realism ('external realism') critically.

First, let me say that one need not be a physicalist to admit that there is something fundamental about 'physical reality'. The question is: What makes it fundamental, and in what sense? As we shall see below, I answer this question very differently from Searle.

Second, while there is a genuine distinction between physical and social reality, it does not amount to the absolute distinction Searle makes it out to be.

Third, let me note what I think Searle also appreciates, viz. that there are two different senses in which the term 'reality' is used. In one of these, the term is used *within* a particular form of discourse. Thus, in connection with physical things, for instance, we may say of what is shimmering in the distance that it is *really* water, that what we see there is *real* and not a mirage, an illusion. This is clearly an important contrast, which we draw within a form of discourse. The other sense, associated with philosophical talk of *physical reality*, refers to the logical space itself within which we distinguish what is real from what is not, what is true from what is false, what is a fact from what is not. Thus, to take an example from Searle: the existence of Mount Everest or, for that matter, its non-existence (as a supposition), its having or not having snow and ice on its summit, would count as facts, or possible facts, within the logical space which constitutes the dimension of physical reality – the dimension of the world in which we live.

As I said, Searle appreciates this. He points out that what G. E. Moore set out to prove, namely the existence of physical objects as such – unlike the continued existence of a building which has escaped the bulldozers – is not an empirical claim. It is, as Searle puts it, 'a purely formal [claim] without any specific content'.[56] Thus, the way in which the claim that the building in question has not been destroyed but still stands (and hence exists) is to be established is very different from the way in which the claim that Mrs N. still loves her husband, that his infidelity has not destroyed her love for him, is to be established or supported. This difference belongs to, or is part of, the difference between the two different forms of discourse in question. It is a difference in the way we distinguish between what is real and what is only apparent or illusory, within two different dimensions of reality. It is, therefore, 'a purely formal' matter concerning 'conditions of intelligibility' pertaining to different forms of discourse. That is why, as Searle rightly points out, you cannot establish the existence of physical objects or their reality as such, without begging the question.[57]

So far, so good. This applies to *all* forms of reality marked by what Wittgenstein calls 'formal' or 'logical' concepts, such as mind, matter, time and number, etc., as opposed to what he calls 'ordinary' or 'empirical' concepts such as 'the thought that . . .', 'house', 'hand', 'apple' and '5 o'clock'.[58] (Not only 'number' in general, but particular numbers are formal concepts.) However, having gone this far, Searle either does not, or is unable to, embrace the full implications of what he has already acknowledged about the different senses of 'reality'. He makes an exception in the case of physical reality, which he detaches from the language or form of discourse that gives it its logical character. What prompts him to do so is his distinction between a 'social construction' involving a language and its speakers, and that which is not only 'logically independent of any human institution' but 'logically prior to them'.[59]

Searle represents what is 'socially constructed', Y, as 'X counts as Y in context C' – e.g. X, a bit of paper, becomes money, Y, when we impose on it an institutional status, given certain legal and social circumstances.[60] These circumstances involve agreement between those who belong to a particular society.[61] As Searle sees it, X will ultimately be a thing or certain phenomena, the existence of which does *not* involve human agreement and is thus totally independent of us. Searle talks here of a brute, language-independent, existent. As he puts it: 'Take away all language and Mt. Everest still has snow and ice near the summit'.[62] And also: 'It is only from a point of view that we represent reality, [whereas] ontologically objective reality does not have a point of view'[63] – i.e. it 'exists without our system of concepts',[64] unrepresented. Or to put it differently again: We take X, a bit of paper or metal, as a coin or paper money, Y, or see it under such an aspect.

Earlier on, I noted Searle's observation that 'even if we don't have words for "man", "line" and "ball" we can see that man cross that line [in a football pitch] carrying the ball',[65] but that this is not so in the case of the six points counting as a touchdown. An animal too, a dog for instance, cannot see points the way it can see the cat up the tree. I should like to point out that this is to take too narrow a view of language. Isn't a ball an inflated piece of rubber in spherical shape? And what about the things we do with it? Do these not also characterize its identity? As for the dog who recognizes what it sees in the tree as a cat, does this not presuppose some learning? Does it not come to respond or react to a cat in the environment in which it grows up from puppyhood? Does it not recognize the cat as the object of such responses?

We can see that, on Searle's account, the hierarchy of Xs must eventually bottom out. But what does it bottom out into ultimately? What is this raw material? The way Searle thinks is as follows: We may make a map of a particular corner of the world in different ways. This particular corner of the world exists independently of the maps and of us, the makers and users of maps. Take another example, this time mine: Eskimos have, I believe, 20 different names for types of snow – many more than we do. Presumably, the raw material, the unconceptualized brute matter, is, in the one case, a particular corner of the world, and in the other it is snow. But do these – a corner of the world, snow – have an identity independently of our concepts? Are we not dealing with classes here, with what we have classified as snow, for instance? And if I have not been fair to Searle in these examples, where does the ultimate bottoming out, the ultimate terminus, occur? What is this unclassified thing that we map or divide up in different ways?

To repeat, do the words or expressions 'the man', 'the ball', 'the line' and 'the Evening Star' refer to language-independent objects? Can anything we can think of, identify, classify, or refer to, be independent of a language and of everything that the existence of a language presupposes?

Beyond that, all we can find is 'an unknown somewhat', if that means anything! Going back to our earlier example of the Eskimos' talk of snow, the 'language-independent reality that can be carved up or divided in different ways by different vocabularies' is, therefore, either the snow which they describe in different vocabulary from ours and which clearly does not come unconceptualized; or it is 'an unknown somewhat', a philosopher's myth, something of which no sense can be made.

Searle writes: 'A socially constructed reality presupposes a reality independent of all social constructions, because there has to be something for the construction to be constructed out of'.[66] He is being misled here by an inappropriate analogy. A house is constructed out of bricks – a manufactured product. Bricks are constructed, let us say, out of earth and sand, its *raw materials* found in nature as such. But why should the materials used in constructing 'institutional objects', in the way Searle suggests, need to be 'absolutely raw'? Why should they not be found in and picked out of the world of our language? Why must the bottoming out go beyond that?

To the philosophical sceptic who searches for an *ultimate* justification, without being able to escape the vicious circle noted by Hume, Wittgenstein says: 'justification comes to an end'.[67] Searle himself points out that the kind of proof used by Moore to answer the sceptic's doubts is inevitably question-begging. Why should this not be true of the 'bottoming out' which Searle takes to be characteristic of 'the construction of social reality'? Let me put it this way: let us not, for the moment, question Searle's idea that social reality is a human construction. Why should we imagine that such a construction must begin in a social vacuum? Indeed, I would much rather think of social reality as the result of an historical development to which human beings can and do make various contributions. Clearly, such contributions take place – and are only possible – in a cultural, historical setting.

Searle writes: 'Public language presupposes a public world.' I would rather say that 'public language' (what other kind is there?) gives us a public world, or rather that a public world is inseparable from a 'public language'. Again, Searle says: 'A socially constructed reality presupposes a non-socially constructed reality.' I do not know what he means by a non-socially constructed reality. I think that what he wants to say (and what he has, in fact, said) is that a socially constructed reality presupposes – bottoms out into – an unconstructed or 'brute' reality. I have just pointed out that this is a symptom of the kind of faulty reasoning with which we are familiar in philosophy.

Recall Searle's claim: 'Take away all language and Mt. Everest still has snow and ice near the summit.' If this means: take dynamite and blow up all inhabitants, or at least all human beings, on this planet, thus removing all speech and so all language from it, and Mount Everest will still be there with snow and ice near its summit, then it is obviously true. But what is true here is a prediction, a claim in the future tense, or perhaps better a hypothetical claim of the form 'if so-and-so, then such-and-such'. And that claim clearly presupposes language. Put it like this: what is predicated or supposed in this example, namely snow and ice near the summit of a mountain, is and must be within the realm of the possible. It is and must be something that makes sense and is, therefore, something we can understand. And that this should be so presupposes language. This is what makes it thinkable. Thus, when Searle writes that 'ontologically objective reality does not have (or better does not presuppose) a point of view' he is clearly wrong; there can be no such reality. To return to the snow and ice on Mount Everest: in what he says Searle is asking us to agree to something which, at the same time, he renders unthinkable by removing it from the realm of the possible.

Let me put it yet another way, for the point bears on other things Searle says. When we speak about Mount Everest and say that in such-and-such circumstances it will still have snow and ice near its summit, we are speaking from within our world, the world of our language, with its past and future. Realists like Searle have unsuccessfully tried to make the same point by referring to the past before there were any human beings on earth, and so any language. Were there not dinosaurs then? Of course there were. What we claim in both these cases, i.e. times past and future, when there either were or will be no people and hence no language, falls within the logical space encompassed by the world of our language. In neither case are we, therefore – and contrary to Searle – 'taking away all language'.

'The world of our language, indeed of any natural language', let us be clear, is the logical space of possibilities, of what makes sense. I think Searle would agree that the world understood in this sense is not a place, although there is a sense in which it means 'the earth' – hence the title of Jules Verne's novel, *Around the World in Eighty Days*. So, in the sense that concerns us, when we say, 'He lives in another world', 'world' does not refer to *where* he lives; just as when we say of someone lost in his thoughts, 'He does not seem to be here with us', 'here' does not designate the place where he stands. We are referring to the preoccupations that cut him off from the diverse engagements that bind together those around him. That world is everywhere infused with the language we and our neighbours speak, and with the forms of significance grounded in that language – forms of significance from which the identity of the objects of our responses cannot be divorced. This is, of course, also true of the world of people who have, perhaps temporarily, lost touch with their neighbours. That world is also a slice of the public world from which they have been segregated, perhaps distorted by their fantasies – fantasies in which the language they share with others enables them to indulge.

Let me return to the question of how we are to conceive of the fundamental characters which Searle attributes to physical reality. I do not disagree with the claim that physical reality has a fundamental character. But what gives it this character? Searle's answer, as we have seen, is expressed within the framework of his realism and physicalism. Thus, he thinks of the relation between mental and physical reality in terms of 'how ... mental reality, a world of consciousness, intentionality, and other mental phenomena, fit into a world consisting entirely of physical particles in fields of force.'[68]

Now, the world of science is certainly part of the world of our language, but that is not the way Searle thinks of it. For him, strangely, physical reality, conceived of as brute and independent of language, coincides with its representation through the atomic theory of matter. I say 'strangely', since its being represented by a theory – its being representable at all – should, according to Searle, exclude its independence from language. Anyway, in contrast to Searle, I think of the relation between mind and matter in the context of the behaviour and responses of a flesh-and-blood being – i.e. a creature whose being participates in physical reality – in the circumstances of a life lived with language. The body that is in question here is seen under a very different aspect from the one presented by Searle, for he thinks of it as the anatomical body of sinews, and nerves and inner organs with their various physiological functions. Those parts of the body which, under this aspect, have these functions, ultimately consist of 'physical particles in fields of force'. All this is important for biological and medical purposes. By contrast, the aspect under which the body is seen to be displaying the mind, either with the person's consent or unwittingly, is the body-in-motion of a living person with a face and eyes, a person capable of gestures, facial expressions and speech.

This is what I mean when I say that a person is a flesh-and-blood being, in contrast to Descartes, who speaks of a person as a thinking thing (*res cogitans*). Searle, like other materialists, goes to the opposite extreme. For him, the mind, consciousness, etc., is a causal consequence of the physiological processes of the body which, for Descartes, is an instrument of the mind, the thinking thing – even though he says that the two are indissolubly mixed.

Anyhow, my point is that the physical existence of human beings as conscious intentional agents is one instance where the fundamental character of physical reality can be seen. Clearly, Searle and I radically disagree over what this physical existence comes to.

I equally differ from Searle about the place and character of physical reality in social life. As we have seen, Searle thinks that physical reality enters social reality as its ultimate foundation and as the raw material on which its construction rests. In contrast, I think that social reality cannot be divorced from physical reality, insofar as the human agents in society are flesh-and-blood beings and, as such, have a physical existence. This is also the case insofar as the surroundings of their actions involve physical reality. But while these surroundings are suffused with modes of significance whose source lies in the language of the society in question, one cannot always extract these modes and get to a purely physical residue, let alone a residue of raw, unconceptualized matter. Indeed, I have rejected the idea of an unconceptualized physical reality, one that is language-independent.

In short, I think of social reality as supplying the framework of human relationships and actions, as part of the human world; and of physical reality as a central part of that framework. Thus, both physical and social reality are language-dependent. They are dimensions of the world of our language. Together with the other dimensions of reality, they form a unity and constitute its wharf and woof. That unity is the unity of a natural language.

Does this make the various dimensions of reality dependent on us? No. This reality and the world of our language exist independently of each and every one of us. Indeed, our world expands from our early childhood onwards as we learn to speak and think, progressively coinciding with the world of adults who share the language we learn to speak. What we thus encounter, and what becomes part of our world, existed before we were born and will continue to exist after we die. This, however, does not mean that the world we come to is immune from change. It is not. For the world of our language, together with that language and its logic, has its temporal dimensions. Within that world, we have a history, and so does the language we speak. Let me note in parentheses that animals, too, share this world, if only partially and to varying degrees. They do so in their instinctive reactions as well as in their learned responses to human beings when they come to share the lives of those they live with – domesticated dogs, for instance.

I said that the world exists independently of each of us, and that we come to it progressively in the process of our development. So, we clearly do not 'construct' any part of it, even though some of us *make a contribution* to the historical and cultural changes that shape the world in which we live. But those who make such contributions do so as creatures who belong to the world they share with others. For it is within that world that we find our being and the capacities that are inseparable from that being. It is only *as such* that we can contribute to changes in the world that mark its history. Thus, neither language nor reality could be said to be constructed by us or described as man-made. Rather, it is we who are largely the product of our language and of the culture in which it is embedded.

So much, then, for Searle's dichotomy between brute physical reality and constructed social reality. I now turn once more to his realism – his 'external realism'. I ask whether agreeing with Hume, as I do, on the continued and independent existence of physical objects, makes one a realist? Does Searle, in his realism, do more than assent to the continued and independent existence of physical objects? I think he does. What makes me hesitate a little is Searle's clear statement that 'external realism is not a thesis or an hypothesis, but the condition of having certain sorts of theses or hypotheses',[69] that 'ER is a background presupposition and not an empirical theory'.[70]

However, as we have seen, Searle clearly detaches the continued and independent existence of physical objects, that is the logical character of physical reality, which he seems to acknowledge in the sentences I have just quoted, from the world of human languages and the agreement which underlies it. In other words, he denies that the *independent* existence of physical objects is *dependent* on human language and the reactions which that language extends – reactions that we have in the case of animals, too. I suppose this seems to Searle a contradiction in terms – as if what you give with one hand you take away with the other. However, no such contradiction is involved here. Physical objects exist independently of *us*: when I shut my eyes, the table on which I have been writing does not disappear, even though my perception of it does. This is a *logical* or *conceptual* difference between physical objects and our sensory perceptions of them. When we say that what we see in the distance is really water, and not a mirage, the claim that what we see is real is *empirical*; but what makes us say, rightly, that what we see is real, the criterion we use in making that claim, is not empirical. It belongs to the logic of the reality of physical objects, and their independence is part of that. So, that physical objects exist independently of us, is part of their logic, a matter of the logical space they occupy in the world of our language. That logic, however, cannot be independent of *language* – the language in which we speak of, or refer to, what has a physical existence.

When Hume said that physical objects have a continued and independent existence, he was commenting on our *conception* of physical reality. He was not making a (true or false) empirical claim, but, as Wittgenstein would say, a *grammatical* remark. The grammar on which Hume is commenting belongs to a particular form of discourse, however pervasively it may enter into other forms of discourse – e.g. when we say of someone, who obviously exists physically, that he has a brilliant mind, or that he is angry.

What a grammatical remark articulates is the *form* of the language we use in saying something, not its *content*, i.e. what we say. The latter may be true or false, and is in any case independent of what we claim; but the form or grammar is what makes it possible for us to claim what we do claim, be it true or false. It is the form of the instrument of language which enables us to make the kind of claim we make. Clearly, that form cannot be separated from the language and all that makes it the kind of language it is. To try to do so would be like trying to separate the human soul from the human body – i.e. from the flesh-and-blood being whose life involves sentience, feeling, and thought – in short: a human being.

Let me finish with a short paragraph that concludes my book *Wittgenstein's Copernican Revolution*, and one in which I summarize – an impossible task, of course – what I attempt to spell out more fully in the book:

> The life we live is a life of the language we speak; and the world in which we live is a world of that life – the life of our language. The structures inherent to its dimensions of reality reflect the grammatical forms of our language – 'grammar' in the sense in which Wittgenstein uses this term. That language has evolved in the course of men's adaptation to and engagement with their environment; and that environment itself, in turn, comes to be increasingly permeated by the forms of significance originating in the course of the evolution of their language. It is in this sense that the human world, the world in which we live, is the world of the life we live with language.[71]

Notes

1   John Searle, *The Construction of Social Reality* (London: Penguin, 1995), xi.

    Editorial Note: John Searle has recently published *Making the Social World* (Oxford: Oxford University Press, 2010). Ilham Dilman died in 2003. Had he lived, he might well have wished to refer to it when commenting on Searle's 1996 volume.

2   Ibid., xi–xii

3   Ibid.

4 Ibid.
5 Ibid., xii
6 Ibid., xii–xiii
7 Ibid., 2.
8 Ibid.
9 Ibid., 55–6.
10 Ibid., 6.
11 Ibid.
12 Ibid., 7.
13 Ibid., 59.
14 Ibid., 61.
15 Ibid.
16 Ibid., 62.
17 Ibid., 66.
18 Ibid., 66–7.
19 Ibid., 68.
20 Ibid.
21 Ibid., 69.
22 Ibid., 70.
23 Ibid., 71.
24 Ibid., I have changed the word 'stones' to 'mountains'.
25 Ibid., 69.
26 Ibid., 69–70.
27 Ibid., 73.
28 Ibid., 75.
29 Ibid.
30 Ibid., 149.
31 Ibid.
32 Ibid., 153.
33 Ibid., 160.
34 Ibid., 161.
35 Ibid., 164.
36 Ibid., 165.
37 Ibid.
38 Ibid., 166.
39 Ibid., 175.
40 Ibid., 176.
41 This is Chapter 8 in Searle's book.
42 Ibid., 178.
43 Ibid.
44 Ibid., 183.

45 Ibid., 184.
46 Ibid.
47 Ibid.
48 Ibid., 186–7.
49 Ibid., 190.
50 Ibid.
51 Ibid., 190.
52 Ibid., 190–1.
53 Ibid., 191.
54 Ibid.
55 Ibid.
56 Ibid., 178.
57 Ibid., 183.
58 See Ludwig Wittgenstein, *Tractatus Logico-Philosophicus*, trans. D. F. Pears and B. F. McGuinness (London: Routledge & Kegan Paul, 1969), § 4.126.
59 Searle, *The Construction of Social Reality*, 183.
60 This is Searle's example.
61 Ibid., 55–6.
62 Ibid., 61.
63 Ibid., 176.
64 Ibid., 166.
65 Ibid., 68.
66 Ibid., 190.
67 Ludwig Wittgenstein, *On Certainty*, ed. G. E. M. Anscombe and G. H. von Wright, trans. Denis Paul and G. E. M. Anscombe (Oxford: Blackwell, 1998)
68 Searle, *The Construction of Social Reality*, xi.
69 Ibid., 178.
70 Ibid., 183.
71 Ilham Dilman, *Wittgenstein's Copernican Revolution* (London: Palgrave, 2000), 218–19.

3 A Critical Examination of Philippa Foot's Recent Account of Moral Judgement

I am going to base my remarks on Philippa Foot's little book *Natural Goodness* and will start by giving an account of her argument. In my exposition, I shall try to be as fair as I can.

A. Exposition
1. *An Objective and Naturalistic Theory of Value Judgement*
In her Introduction, Philippa Foot says that she is interested in the grammar of 'good' as a moral epithet and that she is going to write about what may conveniently be called 'natural goodness and defect in living things'.[1] She elaborates: 'My general thesis is that moral judgement of human actions and dispositions is one example of a genre of evaluation, itself actually characterized by the fact that its objects are living things'.[2]

Foot argues that moral judgements have the same 'conceptual structure' or grammar as 'evaluations of characteristics and operations of other living things'. She divides living things into two classes: those that she characterizes as 'sub-rational', namely plants and animals, and those that are 'rational', namely human beings. There is much about human beings that is subject to evaluation, without the respective judgements being moral judgements – e.g. He has *good* eyesight. Foot talks of such judgements as making 'biological evaluations'. Moral judgements, on the other hand, she takes to be confined to the will – the 'rational will', as she calls it. By 'rational', she means 'responsive to reason'. Thus, her thesis is that moral judgement is essentially 'action-guiding'.[3] Foot is here talking of 'practical rationality', by which she means that morality has to do with 'reasons for acting'.

It is in this dimension, she argues, that we shall find what is distinctive about moral judgements. Still, she holds, such judgements share a common 'grammar' or 'conceptual structure' with the evaluation of all other living things – the endurance of a cactus in a desert climate, the ability of a lion to hunt, the capacity of a root to absorb from the soil nutrients for a plant. In all these examples goodness is contrasted with defectiveness. Foot calls this goodness 'natural goodness'. She also characterizes the norms to which it is answerable in the judgements we make about living things, their characteristics and behaviour, as 'natural norms' – 'natural' because they are used in evaluating 'an individual living thing in its own right, with no reference to *our* interests or desires'.[4] To quote one of her examples: 'It matters in the reproductive life of the peacock that the tail should be brightly coloured'.[5] It matters – so its absence is a *defect* and its presence is a *good*. Foot writes:

> Judgements of goodness or badness can have, it seems, a special 'grammar' when the subject belongs to a living thing, whether plant, animal or human being . . . I think that this special category of goodness is easily overlooked, perhaps because we make so many evaluations of other kinds, as when we assess non-living things in the natural world, such as soil and weather, or again assess artefacts made by humans as are houses and bridges, or made by animals as are the nests of birds or beavers' dams. But the goodness predicated in these latter cases . . . is what I should like to call secondary goodness.[6]

When she says 'easily overlooked', Foot is, I believe, thinking of some of her earlier views. So, even though she is departing from some of these, she is not making a *radical* break from them. Foot characterizes her account of evaluations relating to living things as 'cognitivist' and 'objectivist'. She contrasts her 'naturalism' with G. E. Moore's 'antinaturalism', and her 'cognitivism' with both Stevenson's 'emotivism' and Hare's 'prescriptivism', which she regards as forms of 'subjectivism'. She writes: '*The fact* that a human action or disposition is good of its kind will be taken to be simply *a fact* about a given feature of a certain kind of living thing'.[7] For example, the fact that someone has an honest relationship with his wife is a good thing. That it is a good thing is itself *a fact*. In what sense is it a fact?

Philippa Foot has a detailed argument in support of her contention. She says that 'it is necessary for plants to have water, for birds to build nests' and refers to such necessities as 'Aristotelian necessities'.[8] 'Such necessities', she observes,

> depend on what the particular plants and animals *need*, on their natural habitat, on the ways of making out that are in their repertoire. These things together determine what it is for members of a particular species to be as they *should* be, and to do that which they *should* do.[9]

'What they should do': in other words, what is *good* for them. This is Foot's idea of natural goodness. She then adds: 'And for all the enormous differences between the life of humans and that of plants or animals, we can see that human defects and excellences are similarly related to what human beings are and what they do'.[10] Prior to this, she refers to a paper by Elizabeth Anscombe, 'On Promising and its Justice'.[11] There, Foot says, Anscombe 'points out facts about human life that make it necessary for human beings to be able to bind each other to action through institutions like promising'.[12]

Presumably, the idea is that this is what makes keeping one's promises, one's reliability or trustworthiness, a good thing, a natural good. Foot says that, like wolves which hunt in packs, we are social animals and depend on each other. We do so in virtue of various conventional arrangements. Thus, we act in ways that will benefit others, as others do to benefit us. Presumably, again, this is what makes helping others a natural good. Foot adds that there is clearly something wrong with a free-riding wolf who eats but does not take part in the hunt. Such individuals are just as *defective* as those who have defective hearing, eyesight, or powers of locomotion. Foot says: 'I am, therefore, quite seriously, likening *the basis of moral evaluation* to that of the evaluation of behaviour in animals'.[13] She finds the difference in the fact that human beings are rational animals. A human being, for instance, 'can and should understand that, and why, there is a reason for, say, keeping a promise or behaving fairly'.[14] Foot continues:

Anyone who thinks about it can see that for human beings the teaching and following of morality is something necessary. We can't get on without it. And this is the hub of the proper answer to the challenge: why should it be thought rational to follow morality, but not to obey duelling rules or silly rules of etiquette.[15]

She adds: 'Moral judgement speaks of what there is reason to do'.[16] Further along, she says that 'the grounding of a moral argument is ultimately in facts about human life – facts of the kind that Anscombe mentioned in talking about the good that hangs on the institution of promising.'[17] Foot gives the following kind of examples:

Nobody would, I think, take it as other than a plain matter of fact that there is something wrong with the hearing of a gull that cannot distinguish the cry of its own chick, as with the sight of an owl that cannot see in the dark. Similarly, it is obvious that there are objective, factual evaluations of such things as human sight, hearing, memory and concentration, based on the life form of our own species.[18]

'Why then', she asks, 'does it seem so monstrous a suggestion that the evaluation of the human will should be determined by facts about the nature of human beings and the life of our own species?'[19] Her answer seems to rely on the parallel she sees between 'good sight' and 'good choice'. The function of the eye is to see; that of the will, to choose. An owl hunts in the dark; therefore, if it can see in the dark, we would say it had good sight. Similarly, the will is what we use in making choices. A human being is a rational animal. Therefore, if a person can choose rationally, he makes good choices. Foot concludes that 'moral action is rational action'.[20]

In the chapter on 'Natural Norms' (Chapter 2), Foot concentrates on plants and animals. She finds it natural to contrast goodness with *defect*. A plant that does not grow properly is 'diseased', she says.[21] So is a lioness that is 'a neglectful parent'. 'The individual plant, lioness . . . is weak, diseased or in some other way defective'.[22] Similarly, there is 'something wrong' with a bee that does not dance.[23] The deer is an animal whose form of defence is flight. So, swiftness is a good for the deer, and being slow of foot is a defect.[24] A tortoise, in contrast, has a shell to protect it. So in its case slowness is not a defect; it does not need swiftness to run away from predators. Thus, what counts as good and what counts as a defect is relative to the species.

'In any case', Foot writes, 'the norms we have been talking about so far have been explained in terms of *facts* about things belonging to the natural world'.[25] That is why she talks about 'factual evaluation', 'natural norms', and 'natural goodness and defect'. It is not what *we* approve or recommend that is in question. We are thus dealing with facts, with what is objectively there, facts concerning what an individual needs for development, self-maintenance, and reproduction. It is these facts, Foot says, which determine 'the way an individual *should be*'.[26] Another way she puts it is by saying that the *norms* of our evaluations *are derived from* the life cycle of the species to which the individual belongs.[27] 'By the application of these norms to an individual member of the relevant species it [the individual] is judged to be as it should be or, by contrast, to a lesser or greater degree defective in a certain respect'.[28]

2.   Transition to Human Beings and Moral Judgement

Foot starts with the question 'whether the same structure of judgement is to be found as we move first from plants and animals to human beings, and then from the evaluation of human characteristics and operations in general to the special subject of goodness of the will'.[29] In her view, there is *'no change in the meaning of "good" between the word as it appears in "good roots" and as it appears in "good dispositions of the human will"'*.[30] She writes that 'the common structure of evaluation appears to be unaffected' by the radical difference between plants (which do not have any desires or appetites) and animals (which do) in the 'sub-rational world'. Foot asks: 'But how could we possibly see human good in the same terms?'[31] She continues by saying that in human beings

> the teleological story goes beyond a reference to survival itself . . . The idea of human good is deeply problematic. One may be inclined to think of it [the end towards which people strive in life] as happiness, but much would have to be said before that could be so understood as to be true.[32]

Even so, Foot believes, 'it is possible to give some quite general account of human necessities, that is of what is quite generally needed for human good, if only by starting from the negative idea of human deprivation.'[33] In this connection, she mentions the kinds of things we acquire as part of our normal development, such as learning a language, which enables us to participate in, indeed to entertain, those aspects of human life without which we would be 'deprived individuals', as autistic people are deprived of some of the ingredients that typically belong to the life of a human being. Foot calls the lack of these ingredients 'human defects'. They correspond to the natural defects which we may find in plants and animals. They are defects relative to possibilities without which an individual is deprived. Deprived of what? Having a richer, more complete human life? The benefits offered, or made possible by, human life? Deprived of what is needed for flourishing in human life? I am not clear what Foot's answers to these questions would be.

I shall return to this matter. It is, however, clear that Foot calls the things we are deprived of 'human goods'. A life in which we are not deprived of them, she describes as 'a good human life'. She writes: 'It is therefore possible that the concept of a good human life plays the same part in determining goodness of human characteristics and operations that the concept of flourishing plays in the determination of goodness in plants and animals'.[34] 'So far', she adds, 'the conceptual structure seems to be intact'.[35] It is at this point that she asks whether there is any reason to think that this same conceptual structure should not be in place in our moral judgements.

Earlier in her text, Foot quotes Peter Geach's remark, 'Men need virtues as bees need stings.'[36] She now says that Geach was right:

> Men and women . . . need the ability to form family ties, friendships and special relations with neighbours. They also need codes of

conduct. And how could they have all those things without virtues such as loyalty, fairness, kindness, and in certain circumstances obedience?[37]

Human beings *need* the virtues, 'they play a *necessary* part in the life of human beings as do stings in the life of bees'.[38] Foot describes virtues as 'dispositions of the will', and these, she says, are determined by 'quite *general facts* about human beings'.[39] Thus, she speaks of the good that hangs on trustworthiness and honesty, for instance.[40]

What is the relation between such goodness and what Foot calls 'the necessities of human life'? She thinks that this relation is similar to the one we find in plants and animals: this oak tree has good roots – they are sturdy and deep – because otherwise it would not stay upright. It must be capable of staying upright, for otherwise it would not survive. Similarly, human beings must be able to trust each other, for otherwise they would have to watch each other constantly and miss out on many of the riches that human life has to offer. Foot writes: 'The structure of the derivation is the same whether we derive an evaluation of the roots of a particular tree or of the action of a particular human being'.[41] And, further along in the text:

> Human good must indeed be recognized as different from good in the world of plants and animals, where good consists in success in the cycle of development, self-maintenance, and reproduction. Human good is *sui generis*. Nevertheless – a common conceptual structure remains. For there is a 'natural history story' about how human beings achieve this good as there is about how plants and animals achieve theirs.[42]

3. *Morality and Practical Rationality*

This, then, is how Philippa Foot sees moral judgement as being one kind of evaluation among other evaluations of living things and their characteristics and properties. What is distinctive about it is that it is directed to the human will. Foot talks of the human will as the 'rational will' and of human beings as 'rational animals'. In other words, human beings recognize reasons and are responsive to them – in the choices they make and the actions they perform in the particular situations that belong to the kind of life they live. It is this that makes it possible for us to describe some of those actions and choices, viz. those that pay no heed to such reasons, as 'irrational'.

Foot is interested in showing that 'an intrinsic link' [can] be established between moral goodness and *reasons for action*.[43] She believes that the existence of such a link is part of what an objective theory of moral goodness establishes.[44] Her claim is that there is a 'conceptual connection between acting well and acting rationally'.[45] She variously expresses it as 'the coincidence of moral and rational action',[46] 'the rationality of just action or of disinterested justice',[47] and 'the rationality of doing what virtue demands, of following morality'.[48] Foot says, 'there is a reason for, say, keeping a promise or behaving fairly'.[49] And again: 'No one can act with full practical rationality in the pursuit of a bad end',[50] that 'rational choice should be seen as an aspect of human goodness, standing at the heart of the virtues'.[51] Foot holds that 'we have reason to aim at those things at which a good human being must aim', and that this is what the philosophical sceptic questions.[52] She is adamant that 'one who acts badly *ipso facto* acts in a way that is contrary to practical reason'.[53]

In the chapter entitled, 'A Fresh Start?' Foot poses the problem autobiographically by confessing that she found it difficult to establish 'the coincidence of moral and rational action' – in other words, that to act morally *is* to act rationally. By contrast, she had no problem with prudence or self-interest. She asks: 'What . . . is so special about prudence that it alone among the virtues should be reasonably thought to relate to practical rationality?'[54] The answer, she says, is that prudence is clearly in a person's self-interest and that what is in a person's self-interest is what he desires. Foot admits that she had taken it for granted that reasons (for acting) had to be based on an agent's desires. She says, 'I now believe that both the self-interest theory of rationality and the theory of rationality as desire fulfilment are mistaken'.[55] I think she means that she finds the theory too narrow, too restrictive. 'As I see it', she goes on, 'the rationality of, say, telling the truth, keeping promises, or helping a neighbour is *on a par* with the rationality of self-preserving action, and of the careful and cognizant pursuit of other innocent ends; each being a part or aspect of practical rationality'.[56]

She adds that imprudence, for instance, is by definition contrary to rationality, but self-sacrifice is not. To be imprudent is to knowingly and blatantly ignore one's own safety or to put at risk what one wishes to succeed – e.g. some work in which one is engaged and in which one believes. It is clearly irrational to both believe in it, work for its success, and at the same time knowingly to endanger its success. In other words, what is irrational about imprudence is that I knowingly ignore or act against something that I care about. Where self-sacrifice is concerned, however, a case has to be made. How does Foot make it? By arguing for the *objectivity* of moral goodness. This is the idea that human beings *need* virtue, and hence that there are occasions when virtue demands that one forget oneself and think of others, that one put them before oneself. Therefore, a will which on such occasions responds to the demands of virtue or goodness is responding to what reason demands. However, Foot acknowledges that, in making this case, many questions need to be answered. What if I do not care about being a good human being?[57] As rational animals, people will ask, 'Why should I do that?' – especially if they find that what they have been asked to do is distasteful, to the advantage of others rather than themselves.[58] A philosophical sceptic will ask: why should I do what a good person must do?[59] A gangster may ask: why should I not kill someone if I want to, or when it is in my interest to do so, or to 'teach someone a lesson' when he betrays me?[60]

To repeat my earlier quote: 'Like animals, we do things that will benefit others rather than ourselves. There is no good case for assessing the goodness of human action by reference only to the good that each person brings to himself'.[61] And again: 'Men and women need the ability to form family ties, friendships and special relations with neighbours. How could they have all these things without virtues such as loyalty, fairness, kindness, and in certain circumstances obedience?'[62] It is therefore rational, Foot argues, to do what virtue or goodness demands of one. Does this mean, then, that it is just as irrational to be indifferent to this demand as it is to knowingly act against one's desires? I take it that Foot takes herself to be engaging with this question in Chapter 6 ('Happiness and Human Good'), where she is concerned with the relation between virtue and happiness.

4. *Virtue and Happiness*
At the beginning of Chapter 6, Foot clearly states that

> happiness is not the universal aim of action. Brave people choose great and immediate evils such as certain death, in order to rescue or defend others. And even in their choice of lives some reject happiness for the sake of some other goal.[63]

This is perfectly true; and, if I may add, such people may even find happiness in such a life. Indeed, it is not an accident that those who do not seek happiness and immerse themselves in the pursuit of activities which engage their convictions and/or interests, find happiness in a life of this kind.

What is problematic, Foot says, is 'the thought that happiness may be successfully pursued through evil action. For then it would seem, that

there is an independent criterion of rational action'.[64] She adds: 'I shall question the assumption that happiness can be taken *tout court* to be Man's good', and goes on to ask, 'What, then, is the elusive concept of *happiness* that could rightly be given a central role in moral philosophy?'[65] In response, Foot attempts to sketch out a notion of happiness that has a 'dimension of depth'. She says that 'possible objects of deep happiness seem to be things that are basic in human life, such as home, and family, and work, and friendship . . . [and in the case of some exceptional men and women] artistic creation, and exploration of strange lands'.[66] In other words: it is in such things that people find 'deep happiness'.

Foot says, quite rightly, that in looking at the concept of happiness one must go beyond the description of a life of pleasure and contentment.[67] She then asks: What about the conjunction of even the greatest, deepest, happiness with wickedness?[68] In this connection, she mentions the example of a Nazi who ran one of Hitler's death camps and later enjoyed living in Brazil without much thought about the past. Subsequently, however, he became suicidal. Foot adds, 'perhaps there is always a price to pay for wickedness, in real self-esteem or in the possibilities of loving relations with others'.[69] 'How', she continues, 'could Hitler and others around him have had anything more than a sentimental love of children when they were ready to have one single child driven into a gas chamber?'[70] She further asks: What if this commandant of a death camp thought of himself as helping to purify the Aryan race?[71]

Towards the end of the chapter, Foot wonders again whether one can think of a wicked character as having a happy life. She says that there is 'a way of understanding human good and even human happiness that does not allow such a combination'.[72] By way of illustration, she mentions the case of those in occupied France during the Second World War who sacrificed their happiness by refusing to go along with the Nazis: 'They did not see as their happiness what they could have got by giving in. Happiness, they might have said, was not something possible for them'.[73] Foot's conclusion is that 'there is indeed a kind of happiness that only goodness can achieve, but that by one of the evil chances of life may be out of the reach of even the best of men'.[74] In other words, you can be a good person but still be unhappy; but if you are an evil person, you cannot be happy.

5. *The Rejection of Morality*
In the last chapter of her book ('Immoralism'), Philippa Foot considers the rejection of morality: what are we to say about such a rejection if the judgements of morality (or Christian morality, in particular) are *objective*? Why should I be moral? Is it irrational to reject morality? In this connection,

Foot considers Plato's characters Thrasymachus, Glaucon, Adeimantus and Callicles. Is it justice that we seek or only the appearance of justice? If we were strong enough not to be afraid of others, if we could get away with breaking all the rules of morality, would we continue to stick to 'being moral'? Foot considers Nietzsche's view that our so-called moral actions have a hidden shadow-side which gives them a reality very different from the way they appear to us. 'Christian morality, seen like this', Foot writes, 'has a systematic connection not with happiness but rather with frustration.'[75]

'Is charity then really mostly a sham?' she asks. Her answer is that 'sometimes it is'. To say that genuine charity exists, says Foot, is not 'to reject the depth psychology that is more or less taken for granted nowadays'.[76] She rejects the emphasis Nietzsche places on authenticity and self-fulfilment: murder or robbery is not made good by authenticity or self-fulfilment, it is not justified by the fulfilment that murderers may find in the murders or robberies they commit.[77] Thus, in the last chapter Foot defends the possibility of genuine morality, having argued in the penultimate chapter that the wages of evil are unhappiness. The implication here is that the pursuit of evil is irrational.

B.   Criticism
1.   Human Good and Moral Goodness
We have seen that in *Natural Goodness* Foot's main interest lies in the grammar of 'good' as a moral epithet, the 'conceptual structure' of moral evaluation. She is concerned to develop an *objectivist* theory of moral judgement, one according to which judgements evaluate individuals in their own right, with no reference to *our* [the judge's] interests or desires. It is this, she says, that makes evaluation *objective*. Foot finds the possibility of such moral evaluations in their connection with the 'evaluative judgments of the characteristics and operations of other living things'.[78] Hence she talks of 'natural goodness' and its opposite, 'natural defect'. Such goodness is natural, she says, in that it is 'attributable only to living things themselves and their parts, characteristics and operations . . . and depends on the relation of [the individual] to the "life form" of its species'.[79]

Foot speaks of 'human goodness', yet she constantly slips into talking of 'human good', in the sense of what is good for human beings. Her arguments turn on the idea that human beings cannot get on without morality, that they need virtues such as trustworthiness, loyalty, fairness, justice, tenacity of purpose, etc. The lack of such virtues is, therefore, a form of defectiveness. A person who lacks them is like an oak tree without strong roots. Weak roots in such a big tree as an oak is a defect, just as people who suffer from weakness of will are suffering from a moral defect. Those who do not suffer from such defects are good people and do not lack something that is good for them. They act well. Resoluteness is thus part of human goodness.

In using 'good' in this sense, Foot connects good with benefit. She treads carefully: 'The idea of human good', she writes, 'is deeply problematic'.[80] Indeed, 'Given the fantastic diversity of human lives can we really think of a *species-wide* notion of human good at all?'[81] Foot argues that we can. She mentions Wittgenstein who, on his deathbed, told his friends that he had had a good life. Foot comments: 'We accepted Wittgenstein's description of his life as a good life, but to give so troubled a man as an example of one who had flourished would suggest a special philosophical use of the term'.[82] I would say that this is making heavy weather about the meaning of Wittgenstein's words. What Wittgenstein was doing was expressing gratitude for his life as it was nearing its end.

Next, Foot complains that 'there may be an unwelcome whiff of philosophy even in speaking of human good': it involves much 'rarefaction'.[83] She dismisses the word 'flourishing' for having 'too special implications', and concludes that 'we may get a first glimpse of our quarry by considering the concept of *benefit* as this is applicable in the domain of life'.[84] She had said earlier that 'the idea of a good life for a human being, and the question of its relation to happiness, is each deeply problematic . . . [in view of] the diversity of human beings and human cultures'.[85] 'Nevertheless', Foot writes, 'it is possible to give some quite general account of human necessities' in terms of 'the negative idea of human deprivation'.[86] The price an evil person pays is the human deprivation she talked about earlier.

There is no doubt that Foot's argument is careful and subtle. But it is conducted at a highly abstract level and, as a result, overlooks a number of truths which, as far as I am concerned, render her argument untenable. As I said before, Foot equates her notion of what is good for human beings with moral goodness, which is a concept confined to a particular morality – a 'morality of love', a 'spiritual – i.e. unworldly – morality', like Christian morality. Outside the latter, the word 'good' is, as has been said, the most general epithet of commendation. What it commends is not necessarily moral – e.g. 'a good radio', 'a good medical treatment for a particular disease', 'a good eye'. But even when the commendation is moral, what it commends in the particular circumstances varies with the values of the morality in question. 'Goodness', by contrast, belongs to a particular morality and covers a number of interconnected virtues, such as compassion, justice and humility. What Foot says about what 'good' commends and her remarks about 'goodness' do not fit with the reality of the morality to which goodness belongs. As we have seen, she writes:

> We are social animals, we depend on each other as do wolves that hunt in packs . . . Like the animals, we do things that will benefit others rather than ourselves: there is no good case for assessing the goodness of human action by reference only to the good that each person brings to himself. It will surely not be denied that there is something wrong with a free-riding wolf . . . These free-riding individuals of a species whose members work together are just as defective as those who have defective hearing, sight, or powers of locomotion.[87]

She goes on:

> I am, therefore, quite seriously, likening the basis of moral evaluation to that of the evaluation of behaviour in animals . . . The goods that hang on human co-operation, and hang too on such things as respect for truth, etc., are much more diverse and much harder to delineate than are animal goods. [In contrast with animals] a human being can and should understand that, and why, there is reason for, say, keeping a promise or behaving fairly. We all know enough to say: 'How could we get on without justice?', 'Where would we be if no one helped anyone else?' . . . Anyone who thinks about it can see that for human beings the teaching and following of morality is something necessary. We can't get on without it.[88]

Here Foot is rejecting psychological egoism, arguing that moral actions are ultimately based on reasons. In her view, these reasons have to do with our appreciation of the benefits of moral action, with the acknowledgement that what benefits human beings benefits each one of us. But while she is not denying that many people do the right thing without appreciating this, Foot would say, I think, that those who appreciate it are nearer to moral goodness than those who do not. Perhaps she would say, of those who act without such appreciation, that while their actions are not irrational, not contrary to reason, they are merely acting from custom rather than from reason.

Thus, even though she rejects egoism, Foot nevertheless holds that those who act morally, whether they appreciate it or not, serve themselves by serving others. She certainly argues that 'there is a kind of happiness that only goodness can achieve' – at least in favourable circumstances – one that is beyond the reach of an evil person. I conclude from this that, on Foot's view, intelligent, appreciative, rational people see that if they act morally their actions will benefit them. In other words, they appreciate that in acting morally they will benefit from their own actions. I suggest that it follows from this that, unless such people can at the same time be indifferent to such a benefit, they cannot be good people. For, as the saying goes, if I am to be a good person 'my left hand must not know what my right hand gives'. In other words, my own benefit must not be part of my motive. My benefit or gain must at most be an unexpected bonus. Or, at least, I must be indifferent to such a benefit. So, when Foot says that there are good reasons for being moral, for helping one's neighbours, and that a rational person appreciates this, she is sailing close to and not far from offering us a sullied idea of moral goodness. I shall return to this issue in the next section.

When Foot stresses such things as 'the goods that hang on human co-operation . . . on respect for truth', she clearly means that these things are good for social life, the kind of life on which each of us is dependent. It is this, she argues, that makes them good things. On this account, their good-ness becomes *instrumental* – what is their function? What good do they do? How should they be constituted, so that they can serve this function, do such-and-such good to the species? What must they be like in order to achieve this?[89] Foot writes:

> The common structure of evaluation between botanical and zoologi-cal subjects seems unaffected by the radical difference between the two. It is true, for example, that an answer to a 'Why?' question about an animal may be in terms of appetite and therefore not just about what it needs, but also about what it wants . . . Yet we find the same structural terminology as of goodness or defect relating to parts, characteristics and operations, and also terms such as 'function' and 'purpose' and expressions such as 'in order to' or 'in order that' in things as different from each other as plants and animals.[90]

She goes on:

> The question remains, however, as to whether once we have made the transition from sub-rational to rational beings we may not need a new theory of evaluation.[91] . . . The idea of human good is deeply problematic . . .[92] Nevertheless, for all the diversities of human life, it is possible to give some quite general account of human necessities, that is, of what is quite generally needed for human good, if only by starting from the negative idea of human deprivation.[93]

There are several confusions here, one of which I have already pointed out: (i) between human good and moral goodness, (ii) between an historical account of the development of forms of morality in a society's culture, and the meaning of a morality's values and the logic of its evaluations, and (iii) between the sense of the term 'life' in relation to plants and animals, and the sense it has in connection with human beings. Thus, for instance, plants are *alive*, even though they have no consciousness and no mind of any kind. Animals, too, are *alive* and also have consciousness, but neither plants nor animals have a *life* in the sense that human beings do. And although 'rationality' is part of the difference, it is not the most important feature to mark that (logical) difference. Much more important is the fact that human life admits of the distinction between a meaningful and a meaningless life. When Wittgenstein said that he had had a good life, this was part of what entered into the meaning of what he was saying: he had had a life in which he had been creative, a life which enabled him to make a significant contribution to the world. My point is that moral goodness can only be found, can only make sense, in a life which admits of such a distinction. This is all relevant to my criticism of Foot's instrumental conception of goodness. I now want to develop this criticism further by turning to the connection she makes between goodness and rationality.

2.   *Moral Goodness and Rationality*

Foot speaks of the 'rationality of doing what virtue demands'.[94] She believes that we have 'reason to aim at those things at which a good human being must aim, as for instance doing good rather than harm to others, or keeping faith'.[95] She continues: 'A human being, as a rational animal, will ask, "Why *should* I do that?", particularly if told that he should do something distasteful that seems to be for the advantage of others rather than himself'.[96]

Let me take up this last remark. It is perfectly true that human beings in such a situation may ask: Why should I do that? But they ask such a question because they have lost their foothold in the morality to which they culturally belong, because they are in the grip of a temptation which drives a wedge between them and that morality, or because they have become alienated from it. The only reason or reasons we can give them are moral reasons, reasons which have stopped weighing with them. It is hoped that the alienation is temporary and that they will find their way back to the perspective they have lost. If, however, they say 'I don't care about acting well', we can say 'You *ought* to', though this will make no difference to them, but we cannot accuse them of irrationality. If they persist with asking 'Why should I?', we have to resort to '*moral* persuasion'.

We may hunt around for something that could touch them morally. But if we cannot find it, this does not show that they lack rationality or are irrational.

Referring to her previous views with regard to the rationality of disinterested justice, Foot says:

> I was, rather scandalously, inclined to restrict [the rationality of disinterested justice] to those whose desires were such as to allow them to be described as lovers of justice. I have, therefore, rightly, been accused by my critics of reintroducing subjectivity at the level of rationality while insisting on objectivity in the criteria of moral right and wrong.[97]

To love justice, I would say, one has to see something in it which one finds *morally* attractive, something that makes one want to give oneself to it. I emphasize: what one sees in it, one sees in *moral* terms. It is on this account that one loves justice. Does this make one's love of justice subjective? Let me take up this last question. What one sees here, so I'm inclined to put it, exists independently of us in moral space. When one comes to love justice in this way, one is changed by it, so that when one fights for justice in the face of some injustice, one is authentic, or oneself, in one's fight.

In this case, what one does, comes from oneself. Here, we can say that justice has assumed a reality which it did not have before. That is, in doing what one does in such a case, one is not simply following a pattern of actions, a pattern that one does not own. In this sense, as I have said elsewhere, justice has a *dual reality*: an *objective* reality, in the sense that it has a place outside and independent of one's culture and morality, and it has also a *personal* reality in that it becomes real for the person who 'lives it' in his life. I say 'personal', not subjective.

The dichotomy 'either objective or subjective' is a metaphysical dichotomy. Confined to what the dichotomy opposes, one is unable to do justice to what one wishes to understand. As I have put it elsewhere:

> Simone Weil has pointed out, as I believe Plato has done, that goodness cannot be copied. This encompasses courage, justice and compassion. That is why moral learning is so different from most other forms of learning. Let me add too that this is why the characterization of morality as 'cognitive' is so inadequate – which is not to say that the emotivist view of ethics does better justice to it. For behind those characterizations lurks the dichotomy which splits the head from the heart, reason from feeling or emotion. Behind this

conceptual split we find an inadequate conception of emotion and a narrow view of reason. It remains true nevertheless that a person's emotions may in reality have remained unintegrated with his reason. In such a case their integration will have to be part of his moral learning and development.[98]

Indeed, moral education is to a large extent an education of the emotions, and it involves a change in one's mode of being. Thus while, contrary to Foot, I would myself speak of a 'love of justice', I would never say that 'it is rational to be just', or 'it is rational to keep one's promises'. For that would suggest something like the following: 'Don't be a fool. If you want to get on in this firm, be sure to respect its rules', or 'It is prudent to heed the traffic regulations; don't be too clever and try to get to your destination five minutes earlier by overtaking other vehicles when the traffic is tight'. Yes, prudence is 'rational' – in the sense in which, if you said that justice was rational, you would be saying something like, 'If you think about it, you will see that if people were to be unjust to others whenever they could get away with it, society would gradually disintegrate'. But this has little to do with why the genuinely just are just.

Imprudence, Foot says, is by definition contrary to rationality, whereas self-sacrifice is not.[99] All right, it is irrational to throw away your life, but self-sacrifice is certainly not throwing away your life. Similarly, when I ask someone who is holding my wife hostage and threatening to kill her, to take me hostage and let her go, my reason for doing so is to save her. This is an instance of self-sacrifice. Does this make self-sacrifice rational? Not in the least. The reason why I sacrifice my life to save her is my love for her. Again, in another case, I may sacrifice my life for a total stranger out of compassion. Self-sacrifice is an expression of such love and compassion; and such love and compassion are neither rational nor irrational. In such a case, Simone Weil speaks of 'la folie de l'amour' (the madness of love). Prudence, even when it is for others – as in the case of a bus driver who checks the temptation to drive fast, so as not to put the life of those in his charge at risk – is rational. But justice, compassion, self-sacrifice are not. To describe them as rational is to emasculate them.

One reason why Foot attributes rationality to moral virtues, moral actions and moral judgements is that she wishes to deny that there is a gap between morally neutral facts and moral judgements. 'It is this gap between ground and moral judgement that I am denying', she says.[100] Indeed, 'No good reason has so far been given for thinking that there is any kind of "logical gap" between a moral judgement and its grounds'.[101] This would be innocuous if the grounds in question were not morally neutral grounds. But that is not the way Foot thinks of the matter. She writes:

> What, then, is to be said about the relation between 'fact' and 'value'? The thesis of this chapter is that the grounding of a moral argument is ultimately in facts about human life – facts of the kind that Anscombe mentioned in talking about the good that hangs on the institution of promising, and of the kind that I spoke of in saying why it was a part of rationality for human beings to take special care each of his or her own future. In my view, therefore, a moral evaluation does not stand over against the statement of a matter of fact, but rather has to do with facts about a particular subject matter, as do evaluations of such things as sight and hearing in animals, and other aspects of their behaviour . . . It is obvious that there are objective, factual evaluations of such things as human sight, hearing, etc., based on the life form of our own species. Why, then, does it seem so monstrous a suggestion that the evaluation of the human will should be determined by facts about the nature of human beings and the life of our own species?[102]

Before answering this question, let us remember the kinds of facts about human life to which Elizabeth Anscombe has drawn attention: 'It is necessary for human beings to be able to bind each other to action through institutions like promising, such as that there are so few other ways in which one person can reliably get another to do what he wants'.[103] But is this why those of us who are honest keep our promises? Is this what makes a person trustworthy, ultimately? I do not think so. If it were, then this would make our values instrumental. It would, in fact, make them 'rational' in the sense to which I objected above: 'If you want to get on in this firm, respect its rules.' This, or something like this, may be the reason why institutions like promising have developed in the course of the history of human societies. It would be an historical, sociological explanation regarding a fundamental cultural development in human societies; but it would have nothing to do with why honest, trustworthy people keep their promises. They are honest and trustworthy because they have regard for certain values. Their regard has to do with what they see, *morally*, in honesty. The question 'Why are people honest, or why do they keep their promises?' is a question that throws doubt on people's honesty, on its genuineness. One answer to such a question would be to ask: 'Is the person I am talking to a spy?'

3. From Biology and Physiology to Morality?

Let me now return to Foot's question, which I promised to answer: Why does it seem so monstrous a suggestion that the valuation of the human will should be determined by facts about the nature of human beings and the life of our own species? She says that 'it is obvious that there are objective, factual evaluations of such things as human sight, hearing, memory, and concentration, based on the life form of our own species'.[104] Foot compares this with examples taken from plant and animal life. We can see, she writes, that despite the enormous differences between the life of human beings and that of plants and animals, human defects and excellences are similarly related to what human beings are and what they do.[105]

Birds of prey can see their quarry on the ground from a great height. If such a bird were short-sighted it would have defective sight. If I were so short-sighted that I had to move a book I was reading up to my face, or use a magnifying glass to read it, you would say that I had defective sight and recommend that I should see an optician. Foot argues that the eye is there for us to see with, and, similarly, the will for us to choose with.

The eye is an organ of sight, but the will is not an organ of choice. We see with our eyes, but we do not choose with our will – at least not in the same sense. The will is simply our capacity to choose, to act. This involves deliberation, which is a form of thinking, of considering reasons, etc. Such capacities presuppose human life, the kind of life we live with language. Indeed, we ourselves are the kind of beings we are because the life we lead is inseparable from our identity as human beings. We are not just alive, we have a life, a life in which the very identity of what we encounter in situations constitutive of that life is impregnated with significances. It is in such situations that we think, deliberate, choose, act, care for things, interact with others, and engage with what we face in those situations. It matters to us how we live. Many of the significances which characterize the situations in which we choose, act, feel concern for and care about what we do and what might happen, are *moral* significances. That is, the objects of our responses often have a *moral* character.

My eyes may be defective, but I have not heard of a defective will. A person may be irresolute, he may constantly change his mind, he may find it difficult to make up his mind, he may be weak-willed. These are not defects of the will; they are failures of the person, in contrast to the case of an old man whose eyes are beginning to fail him. Though it is the person who sees with his eyes, his eyes are not *him*, in the sense that it is *he*, the person, who chooses, intends, acts, cares, and responds.

Where people are genuinely good, their morality goes through them; their goodness is a mode of being in which their love and compassion find expression. This is the kind of love in which others are considered in themselves and respected as human beings in their own right. Such love comes with a commitment to values like justice and compassion. These values give one a *perspective* from which, in certain situations, one has a *motive* for acting in a certain way, or for refraining from actions one may otherwise have wanted to perform. This is a perspective shared by anyone who embraces these values. The significances which characterize the situations in which one has a motive for acting or refraining from acting are, therefore, no more in the agent's fantasy than colours are in the eye of the beholder. They are not something he projects; they form part of the logical space in which the situation in which he acts is apprehended by all who share his values and, therefore, his responses.

In this regard, the values in question exist independently of us and are *objective*, and the significances which they enable us to see characterize the situations in which we act *in reality*. It is those who do not see them who may be said – by those who share the perspective of these values – to be 'morally blind' to them. It is their *moral indifference* which makes them blind. In contrast to what makes one physically blind, the moral indifference in question characterizes one's *mode of being*. One has to change *in oneself*, if one is to have access to the significances that characterize the situations in which a good man has a motive for acting. Such a change requires inner work. It is for this reason that morality, at least a morality of goodness and love, is *personal*. The man with cataracts in both eyes must have his cataracts removed if he wants to be able to see; the morally indifferent person, whether he be evil or not, has to change *in himself* to be able to appreciate what the good person appreciates.

Put it like this: a man who has defective sight will want it corrected. He will go to someone who has the expertise to correct it. He certainly has reason to want it corrected. In Foot's terminology, this is the rational thing to do, as opposed to doing nothing or engaging in some kind of mumbo jumbo. In the case of moral indifference, he will probably have no incentive for wanting to change. But if, for one reason or another, his estrangement from certain relationships makes him realize that his moral indifference lies at the source of such estrangement, he may try to do something about it. However, his reasons for wanting to change in order to obtain what he wants, will not take him very far. He has to be touched in a different way; a mere change of behaviour will not amount to anything more than a change in appearance. This may do the trick – dupe others and satisfy him. Maybe where he couldn't get on with his colleagues at work, he will now find that he can. But this is little more than an adjustment to situations he encounters in the routine of his life, and his satisfaction will be shallow.

I said he has to be touched in a different way: for instance, he may feel sorry for someone he has hurt, or someone who has made him angry may ask for his forgiveness, or he may thank someone who has put himself out for him. Any such experience *may* – I stress the 'may' – awaken something new in him. He will have to go out of his way to pursue it, to go on from there. It is this pursuit that I call 'inner work', a wrestling with himself, with the way he is, with what he gravitates to, a wrestling with his defensiveness, maybe with his smugness or arrogance, with his resentments, or his quickness to take offence. Plato, through Socrates in the *Phaedo*, refers to this as the purification of the soul. The soul is purified from the self – the self that is active in selfishness, not the self one encounters in self-knowledge, which Plato identified with 'moral knowledge'.

I quoted above Simone Weil's remark that goodness cannot be copied. Where it is copied, goodness will be something one puts on, something voluntary, something directed at what one wants, something 'rational', as Foot would say. To repeat, it is something one obtains by something one does – like going to see an ophthalmologist in order to have one's eyes treated, so that one can read more easily. It may take some effort on one's part to do so, but the result comes of itself; one does not enter into the process that leads to it.

In the case of moral learning, the goodness to which one comes becomes part of oneself, and one comes to it by learning to give up what one clings to, namely one's defences, the ego's tendency to expand. One learns this in the course of one's interactions with others, if one is open to them and thus to what is outside one. One learns to give up one's resentments, for instance, by forgiving those whose offences or whose arrogance one resents. Forgiving them, grieving over one's own faults and thoughtlessness and the harm they have caused others, being aggrieved by these in one's remorse, are examples of what I mean by 'inner work'.

Earlier, I spoke of 'mere behaviour', where one's goodness is something copied. Here, by contrast, one's goodness, real goodness, will find expression in one's actions, but those actions will come from oneself. One is oneself in one's goodness. Put it like this: goodness will enter one's being if one gives one's heart to it; *not* through one's rationality. When Aline Solness in Ibsen's play *The Master Builder*, does the right thing, saying 'it is only my duty', this does not make her a good person. Her goodness is false, not genuine; it has overtones of resentment.[106]

What I have tried to show is that when we move from good eyes or defective sight to a courageous choice, to an honest person or a weak-willed rascal, we are no longer operating in the same logical space. If you want to find similarities or continuities between different living things, you had better keep to biological life-sciences, sciences which study what all living things have in common; namely, being *alive*. But not even dogs have a life in the sense in which human beings do. They have appetites, are sexually attracted to other dogs, and want things – for instance, food when they are hungry. Domesticated animals are capable of affection, even a certain kind of understanding and courage. They may show determination in what they pursue. A dog often cares for its master and may face danger to save him when attacked. Perhaps he can even be concerned for his master in a limited sense. He may be said to be loyal to his master. But loyalty is not, and cannot be, something a dog admires. He may try to please his master, but can he want to act well independently of what anybody thinks? Can it matter to him how he lives? No, there is no logical space in his life for morality; the kind of life he has cannot provide such a space. If we say that he is a good dog, we do not mean that he is capable of either goodness or evil.

4.   *Morality and Happiness*

If someone is a good person, must he be happy? Can a wicked person be happy? Can happiness be pursued through good actions? Can it be pursued through evil actions?

Let me say that Foot is much less abstract in her discussion of these questions; she has many good things to say here. Her answer to the first question – must a good person be happy? – is that goodness brings happiness, provided the external circumstances permit it. There is much in life that is outside our control. One may be hit by the death of a loved one, or a change of regime, as a result of which one is imprisoned for the expression of one's beliefs, may destroy one's life and the happiness one had found in it.

Still Foot holds that in the absence of such circumstances goodness does bring happiness. I agree. For it is in turning outwards, in taking an interest in things outside one, in caring for people, in creativeness, in one's work (if one can give oneself to it), that one finds happiness. However, as I have argued elsewhere, happiness cannot be pursued as an end; it is in forgetting oneself that one finds happiness. This happiness is an unsought bonus, as it were.[107]

It is equally true that goodness cannot be pursued as an end. If, for instance, in the genuine remorse one feels, one grieves for the pain and harm one has caused others, one does not have an eye on the relief this will bring. If one seeks goodness for any kind of relief or satisfaction, one is 'double-minded' (in Kierkegaard's terminology), and the reward one seeks will separate one from the goodness which one is instrumentalizing for its attainment. When a person attains some goodness in his generosity towards the needy, in his compassion for those who are hungry, in pain, or oppressed, his goodness is invisible to him, hidden from him.

What about the wicked? Certainly, the wicked can prosper. In the *Gorgias*, Socrates speaks of Archelaus, the Macedonian tyrant, as unhappy. But, as I have argued elsewhere, what Socrates is expressing here is his sorrow for someone as wicked as Archelaus.[108] Socrates is saying something like this: Nothing is worse than being evil, so how can an evil person be happy? This does not mean that Archelaus *feels* unhappy. Until and unless he changes, he will continue to kill or to banish those who oppose him, and he will enjoy exercising his power over them.

It is the same with Sonia in Dostoyevsky's *Crime and Punishment* who, when Raskolnikov confesses to her that he is the one who killed the pawnbroker Alyona Ivanovna and her sister Lizavette, exclaims: 'What have you done – what have you done to yourself? . . . There is no one – no one in the whole world now so unhappy as you'.[109] She calls him unhappy because he has done something terrible. What have you done to yourself, to your soul? You have lost your soul, estranged yourself from spiritual life. She would have said 'from *life*', as does Dostoyevsky. It is the evil Raskolnikov has embraced that Sonia laments in these words. Dostoyevsky comments: 'If fate had only sent him repentance . . . the sort . . . that is accompanied by terrible agony which makes one long for the noose or the river! Oh, how happy he would have been . . .'[110] When, at the end of the novel, Raskolnikov does come to such remorse, Dostoyevsky says that a new life opens up for him:

> In those sick and pale faces [those of Raskolnikov and Sonia] the dawn of a new future, of a full resurrection to a new life, was already shining. It was love that brought them back to *life* . . . They still had to wait for another seven years, and what great suffering, and what infinite joy till then! And he had come back to *life*, and he knew it, and felt it with every fibre of his *renewed being* . . . The convicts who had been his enemies looked at him differently; he had even begun talking to them himself, and they replied to him in a very friendly way . . . Suddenly something seemed to seize him and throw him at her [Sonia's] feet. He embraced her knees and wept . . . He remembered how he used to torment her continually and lacerate her heart . . .

He knew with infinite love he would *atone* for her suffering . . . Life had taken the place of dialectics, and something quite different had to work itself out in his mind.[111]

Let me point out very briefly that, although there is this parallel between Sonia's words, 'what have you done to yourself; oh, there is no man more unhappy than you', and those of Plato's Socrates, there is also a big difference between Raskolnikov and Archelaus. Archelaus enjoys the power he exercises, his ego is inflated with it. Raskolnikov, on the other hand, lives a lonely life, estranged from all sources of sustenance, trying to convince himself, by means of what Dostoyevsky calls 'dialectics', that he has committed a crime only in name. As Dostoyevsky puts it at one point: 'the whole world was dead and indifferent, like the cobblestones on which he walked – dead to him, and to him alone'.[112] Raskolnikov's life had lost all its zest and turned into 'mere existence'. This is clearly the result of his alienation from the morality with which he had grown up since childhood.

What we have here is the kind of thing Foot writes about in the chapter 'Happiness and Human Good'. Without morality, one may have a purpose but not an anchor. As Simone Weil puts it: 'All the passions produce prodigies. A gambler is capable of watching and fasting almost like a saint'.[113] I could add: stop him gambling, and he will go to pieces. It is the satisfaction of his psychological needs that keeps him standing. By contrast, someone who has moral convictions has 'inner strength'. Even in isolation his inner resources keep him standing.

I said that happiness cannot be pursued as an end, nor can good actions be made into a means to happiness without losing their goodness. Can happiness be pursued through evil actions? I do not think that Hitler acted the way he did in order to be happy. He was immersed in what he was trying to achieve, the purification of the Aryan race with which he identified himself. He was driven by his ambitions, by his attempt to prove to himself his own greatness – probably to compensate for early injuries to his self-esteem. I do not think that either Hitler or others would think of Hitler's life in terms of its happiness or lack thereof. Thus, if anyone said that Hitler had been unhappy, or had an unhappy life, he would be saying this in the spirit in which Socrates said this of Archelaus, and he would have to be a saint to say so – compassion for such an evil person is something most of us are incapable of.

5. 'Immoralism'
Why should I be moral? Is it not better to be strong? Can morality be justified? What are Nietzsche's charges against morality, i.e. Christian

morality, or what I have called a morality of love? Is charity mostly a sham, as Nietzsche thought? I have already said something about the first question. Taken together with the second question, what is being asked could be put like this: Why should I turn the other cheek if I am strong? Is it not because I am weak that I do so? In doing so, I appease the strong person and save my face at the same time. Christian morality is a 'slave morality', a morality of the weak. This is what Nietzsche thought. So does Callicles in the *Gorgias*:

> No, no man would put up with suffering what's unjust; only a slave would do so, one who is better dead than alive, who when he's treated unjustly and abused can't protect himself or anyone else he cares about . . . Nature herself reveals that it's a just thing for the better man and the more capable man to have a greater share than they.[114]

One could grant Callicles that the strong person generally does prevail over the weaker, but it does not follow that he *should*. In this connection, Simone Weil opposes what is natural to what is just. Contrasting the natural with the spiritual, which she often calls super-natural, she speaks from *within* Christian morality. She talks of the natural in us pulling us morally down towards baseness, and refers to this pull as 'moral gravity'. To move in the opposite direction, she says, one has to turn away from the self or ego, from that within oneself which has a tendency to expand. Such a tendency is 'natural'. If one turns away from the ego, the goodness towards which one will have turned, she says, will give one wings.[115] One will rise morally. Thus, she juxtaposes moral gravity with grace. I emphasize that she is speaking from *within* a morality of love. But she also sheds light on its content, on what she sees in it.

To return to Nietzsche, he too speaks from *within* his morality (of strength). But the matter is not as simple and straightforward as that. I cannot go into it now, nor do I know Nietzsche's work well enough to do so. The only thing I would point out is that he tends to 'psychologize' Christian morality. First, he thinks that people follow it like a herd, and so he calls it a 'herd morality', a morality of 'the weak and the inferior'. Nietzsche is a loner, someone who thinks for himself. Therefore, what he sees and, in many cases, what he makes of what he sees, fills him with contempt. Second, he is a man with psychological insight, in some ways a precursor of Freud, and behind the exercise of charity he sees a psychological dynamic which falsifies the charitable acts in which people engage.

Foot asks: 'Are those whose compassion for the unfortunate may even go so far as to rule their lives really to be seen as thereby expressing a twisted sense of inferiority? Is charity really mostly a sham?'[116] She answers, correctly, that *sometimes* it is:

> Nietzsche, with his devilish eye for hidden malice and self-aggrandizement and for acts of kindness motivated by the wish to still self-doubt, arouses a wry sense of familiarity in most of us. But this is not to say that there is not a great deal of genuine charity.[117]

I would add: is humility necessarily a form of servility? Of course not. In those cases where it is, it is the opposite of what it appears to be: a form of base self-seeking. As Foot rightly points out: 'Love and other forms of kindness . . . may be a sign of strength rather than weakness in those who are sorry for us.' She adds: 'We may reasonably think . . . that charity makes for happiness in the one who has it, as hardness does not'.[118] I agree. In charity one forgets oneself, whereas the hard person is closed to others. He often has a cynical view of the world. He is thinking of himself, is on the defensive in the way he isolates himself from others. All this militates against the possibility of finding happiness in life.

However, when Foot returns to her hobby-horse, the contrast between 'natural goodness' and 'natural defect', she loses her good sense. I do not think that when Nietzsche denied that 'to pity others is to have a good disposition towards them', he was 'challenging a judgement about . . . natural goodness and defect in the human species'.[119] Foot says that the dancing operation in honey bees plays a beneficial role in the life of the hive. Corpulence was once thought to be good for human beings, before it was realized that it went with ill-health. According to Foot, Nietzsche likewise asked whether pity was good for the one pitying or the one pitied. He was asking, therefore, whether it is a disposition that should be cultivated, rather than avoided in human life.[120] Foot writes: 'I have suggested that he, Nietzsche, got his facts wrong; but if his facts had been right, his revaluation of pity would have been right'.[121]

No, Nietzsche is not asking whether pity is good for one. What he claims is that it is a contemptible disposition. This is partly because he confuses pity with servility, though this is not the whole story. In pity he sees an expression of weakness; the strong man is not deflected from his path by pity. This is itself a *moral* judgement, and a moral judgement is not ultimately founded on facts concerning what makes a disposition good for human beings, in the way that Foot suggests. Between Christianity and Nietzsche there is a moral conflict which cannot be resolved in this way; it is a conflict between two opposing moral values, between two perspectives. There is no neutral vantage point from which such a conflict can be resolved.

As for the questions '*Must* pity or compassion have a psychological underside?', 'Must it be sham?, '*Can* it ever be genuine?': These questions raise *conceptual* issues, as is not the case with, for example, 'Is pity to be despised?', which raises a *moral* question .

Is Nietzsche an immoralist, does he reject morality altogether? I think that what he criticizes and rejects is Christian morality, not morality as such. Insofar as he suggests that all morality has a psychological under-side, he is suggesting that we are deluded, that no moral values are what they appear to be. If this means that all moral values are false, then it is a paradoxical claim, since 'false' here is itself a moral predicate. As for the question, 'Can morality be justified?' I have already said something about it. It is not like the question, 'Can there be a justification for having any traffic rules?' The answer is: 'Yes. Without traffic regulations there would be traffic chaos, and who would want that?' As we have seen, Foot's response to the analogous question about morality, resembles this answer.

But this is wrong. Foot's question is typical of the kind of question the philosophical sceptic asks; for instance, whether induction in itself can be. Or, and this comes to the same thing: can an inductive inference be justified *ultimately*? Foot likewise asks whether morality itself can be justified. What is the *ultimate* justification of our moral judgements, our moral actions and decisions? I have criticized her and I have rejected her answer. Her account of moral judgement, of the kind of morality in which goodness has its home, is way off the mark.

My answer to the above question is that the *ultimate* justification of our moral judgements, decisions and actions is to be found in our moral values. The philosophical sceptic, not satisfied with this answer, asks: and what is the justification of our moral values? Why do we believe in, why are we committed to, the moral values in which we believe and for which we are willing to fight? How are they to be defended? My answer is: by making explicit what we see in them, by spelling out their *moral* appeal to us *personally*. I say 'personally' because each person has to speak for himself here. Wherever this question arises between two people with different values, the first move is to try and find out how much they have morally in common. But in the end, as Wittgenstein said, our reasons – our *moral* reasons – run out, and at the end of reasons comes *persuasion*.[122]

6. Conclusion

Philippa Foot's *Natural Goodness* is a book that is well written, clearly argued, well organized and sophisticated. However, in her philosophical zeal to reject subjectivist, emotivist, non-congnitivist views of the nature of moral judgement and to correct their errors, she develops an equally untenable objectivist, rationalist and cognitivist theory. In the last two chapters of her book she says much that is good and insightful, underlining her sensitivity and perceptiveness. It is interesting, however, that when it comes to mustering philosophical arguments, these qualities are inoperative, that what Foot thus knows and understands, is lost sight of. I repeat, her arguments are ingenious; she displays subtlety and intelligence in developing them. Alas, though, her philosophical tenaciousness prevents her from appreciating what, I am sure, is well within her grasp.

Philosophy is at least partly to blame for this state of affairs. For although philosophy has the capacity to enlighten and to illuminate whatever its questions are directed at, it has also the capacity to mislead. For, as Wittgenstein has pointed out, philosophy is a struggle with illusion, delusion and misapprehension, where these at the same time are its own products.

Notes

1   Philippa Foot, *Natural Goodness* (Oxford: Clarendon Press, 2003), 3.
2   Ibid., 4.
3   Ibid., 9.
4   Ibid., 33.
5   Ibid.
6   Ibid., 26.
7   Ibid., 5, 18.
8   Ibid., 15.
9   Ibid.
10 Ibid.
11 G. E. M. Anscombe, "On Promising and its Justice", in *Collected Philosophical Papers* (Minneapolis, University of Minnesota Press), Vol. 3: *Ethics, Religion and Politics*, 18.
12 Foot, *Natural Goodness*, 15.
13 Ibid., 16. My emphasis.
14 Ibid.
15 Ibid., 16–17.
16 Ibid., 18.
17 Ibid., 24.
18 Ibid.

19 Ibid.
20 Ibid., 24.
21 Ibid., 29.
22 Ibid., 30.
23 Ibid., 35.
24 Ibid., 34.
25 Ibid., 36–7.
26 Ibid., 33.
27 Ibid., 33–4.
28 Ibid.
29 Ibid., 38.
30 Ibid., 39.
31 Ibid., 40–1.
32 Ibid., 43.
33 Ibid.
34 Ibid., 44.
35 Ibid.
36 P. T. Geach, *The Virtues* (Cambridge: Cambridge University Press, 1977), 17.
37 Foot, *Natural Goodness*, 44–5.
38 Ibid. My emphasis.
39 Ibid., 45. My emphasis.
40 Ibid.
41 Ibid., 47.
42 Ibid., 51.
43 Ibid., 64.
44 Ibid.
45 Ibid., 65.
46 Ibid., 9.
47 Ibid.
48 Ibid., 16–17.
49 Ibid., 16.
50 Ibid., 14.
51 Ibid., 81.
52 Ibid., 53.
53 Ibid., 62.
54 Ibid., 63.
55 Ibid., 10.
56 Ibid., 11.
57 Ibid., 52.
58 Ibid., 56.

59 Ibid., 64.
60 Ibid., 65.
61 Ibid., 16.
62 Ibid., 44–5.
63 Ibid., 82.
64 Ibid.
65 Ibid., 86.
66 Ibid., 88.
67 Ibid., 90.
68 Ibid.
69 Ibid.
70 Ibid., Footnote 12.
71 Ibid., 91.
72 Ibid., 92.
73 Ibid., 96.
74 Ibid., 97.
75 Ibid., 157.
76 Ibid., 108.
77 Ibid., 114.
78 Ibid., 25.
79 Ibid., 27.
80 Ibid., 43.
81 Ibid., 92.
82 Ibid., 93.
83 Ibid.
84 Ibid.
85 Ibid., 43.
86 Ibid.
87 Ibid., 16–17.
88 Ibid.,
89 Ibid., 31–2.
90 Ibid., 40–1.
91 Ibid., 41.
92 Ibid., 43.
93 Ibid.
94 Ibid., 53.
95 Ibid.
96 Ibid., 56–7.
97 Ibid., 10.
98 Ilham Dilman, *Wittgenstein's Copernican Revolution* (London: Palgrave, 2002), 198–9.

 99 Foot, *Natural Goodness*, 11.

100 Ibid., 9.

101 Ibid., 20.

102 Ibid., 24.

103 Ibid., 15. See Anscombe, 'On Promising and its Justice', 18.

104 Foot, *Natural Goodness*, 24.

105 Ibid.

106 Peter Winch, 'Moral Integrity', in *Ethics and Action* (London: Routledge, 1972), 180.

107 See Ilham Dilman, *Raskolnikov's Rebirth: Psychology and the Understanding of Good and Evil* (Chicago Ill.: Open Court, 2000), Chapter 5, 'Happiness: Can it Be Pursued as an End?', 79–93.

108 See Ilham Dilman, *Morality and the Inner Life: A Study in Plato's 'Gorgias'* (London: Macmillan, 1979), Chapter 4, 'Virtue and Happiness', 47–70.

109 Fyodor Dostoyevsky, *Crime and Punishment*, trans. Constance Garnett (London: Everyman, 1956), 552.

110 Ibid., 552.

111 Ibid., 557–8. My italics.

112 Foot, *Natural Goodness*, 194.

113 Simone Weil, *Gravity and Grace*, trans. Emma Crawford (London: Routledge, 2002), 55.

114 Plato, *Gorgias*, trans. Donald J. Zeyl, in *Plato: Complete Works*, ed. John M. Cooper (Indianapolis: Hackett, 1997), 483b, d.

115 Weil, *Gravity and Grace*, 4.

116 Foot, *Natural Goodness*, 107.

117 Ibid., 107.

118 Ibid., 105.

119 Ibid., 109.

120 Ibid., 108–9.

121 Ibid., 110.

122 Ludwig Wittgenstein, *On Certainty* (Oxford: Blackwell, 1998), ed. G. E. M. Anscombe and G. H. von Wright, trans. Denis Paul and G. E. M. Anscombe, §612.

4   Donald Davidson I: Human Agency, Action and Intention

I want to comment on the first part of Donald Davidson's collection of essays entitled *Actions and Events*. As in my other discussions, I shall start with a summary of what my author argues. But unlike what I have done previously, I will concentrate on various aspects of what he writes and intersperse my summaries and quotations with comments. The reason for this is twofold. First, we are dealing with individual essays, however much they may be connected. Second, there is a lot of detail, some of which – e.g. where the argument is abstract and one has to refer back-wards and forwards – disinclines me to make the necessary effort. This is a personal confession. But the reason for my reluctance is that, even where I agree with something Davidson says in passing, I do not find the effort rewarding. Is that personal? I am not sure. This is a question I will return to. So, I will start by giving a brief summary of the essays, parts of which I wish to discuss.

1.   Actions, Reasons and Causes

In his Introduction to the essays, Davidson says that the general theme of the collection is 'the role of causal concepts in the description and explana-tion of human action'.[1] The thesis, he says, is that

> the ordinary notion of cause which enters into scientific or common-sense accounts of non-psychological affairs is essential also to the understanding of what it is to act with a reason, to have a certain intention in acting, to be an agent, to act counter to one's own best judgement, or to act freely.[2]

In the first essays, Davidson says that the reason for an action 'rationalizes' the action. The use of this word strikes me as strange after Freud, but what Davidson means is that it makes a person's actions rational. He goes on to add that 'rationalization is a species of causal explanation'.[3] In other words, to give the reason for an action is to give a causal explanation of it. I find this claim startling, to say the least.

However, Davidson points out that a reason 'rationalizes' an action by leading us 'to see something the agent saw, or thought he saw, in his action' – in other words, by taking us into the agent's mind. So, it would seem that a reason must be a special kind of cause. Moreover, the causal relation in question is not a purely external relation. That is, it is not simply a contingent matter that, when agents are in such-and-such a situation, they respond in such-and-such a way or do so-and-so. It is rather that, because of what it means to them or what they see in it, the situation calls for a certain response, demands a certain action from them. But Davidson is not very clear on this point; he speaks of a 'pro attitude', somewhat as one would speak of the positive pole of a battery: 'he [the agent] happens to have a pro attitude towards such-and-such, and that is why he moves towards it'. Thus, 'He does something for a reason' equals 'He has a sort of pro attitude towards actions of a certain kind and he believes that his action is of that kind'.[4]

Again Davidson says: 'giving the reason why an agent did something is often a matter of naming the pro attitude . . . or the related belief . . . or both.'[5] For example, I like sweet things. I believe or know that chocolate is sweet. So I will reach for it and eat it. Davidson talks of such a pro attitude and related beliefs as 'the primary reason'.[6] 'The primary reason for an action', he says, 'is its cause.'[7] He continues: 'Because "I wanted to turn on the light" and "I turned on the light" are logically independent, the first can be used to give a reason why the second is true'.[8] They are logically independent – that is, I can want to do something but not do it. No contradiction is involved here. But is the intelligibility of doing something because one wants to do it, for whatever reason, like that of the water in a puddle evaporating because the air is hot? At this stage, I am merely raising the question against the background of Davidson's identification of reasons for action with causes. He writes: 'To know a primary reason why someone acted as he did is to know an intention with which the action was done'.[9] If I reached for the bar of chocolate because I wanted to eat it, then I reached for it with the intention to eat it. 'But', Davidson adds, 'to know the intention is not necessarily to know the primary reason in full detail.'[10] All right, so I reached for the chocolate with the intention to eat it. Hence I must have had a pro attitude towards eating it. But was this because I was hungry, or because I craved for something sweet, or because I thought I would offend the host who put it in front of me?

I do not know where this is taking us. On page 8 of his book, Davidson distinguishes between the explanatory and the justificatory roles of reason. I am familiar with and understand this distinction, independently of what Davidson writes here. 'Why are you pouring me out a drink?' – 'It will soothe your nerves.' My reason, 'to soothe your nerves', *explains* my action. 'Why should you want to soothe my nerves?' – 'Because I want you to make a good impression during your interview.' This second explanation *justifies* my action. In the last paragraph of Section II, Davidson writes: 'The justifying role of a reason . . . depends upon the explanatory role, but the converse does not hold.'[11] He gives an example: You step on my toes. So I step on your toes in response. Davidson says that what you have done neither explains nor justifies my response, 'unless I believed you stepped on my toes'. He adds, 'but the belief alone, true or false, explains my action'.[12] This is so obviously true that I wonder why Davidson takes the trouble to point it out.

Is there something I have missed? The only point I can think of is this: a Humean cause which explains its effect is not mediated by a belief. Take a knee jerk, for instance. You tap me on the knee and my leg goes up. I do not need to know or to believe that you have tapped me on the knee. It is my *leg* that responds to the tap. *I* have nothing to do with it. But in Davidson's example it is not my foot that responds; it is *I*. For this to be so, I must either know that you have stepped on my toe and therefore want to retaliate, or I must at least think that you have stepped on my toe when you have not. If this is Davidson's point, if he wants to insist that what we have here is the effect of a cause, then he must be working simultaneously with different senses of 'cause'.

As I said earlier, Davidson seems to suggest that if a reason is a cause, then it is a special kind of cause. Here I am not commenting but simply trying to understand, so that I can give as fair a summary of Davidson's position as possible. In the remainder of the essay Davidson briefly considers objections to his view that 'reasons for actions are causes'. He begins by pointing out that there is an anaemic sense in which every rationalization – the giving of reasons for what one has done– justifies an action. This is because 'from the agent's point of view there was, when he acted, something to be said for the action'.[13] I do not see this. 'I did it, because I thought it would please me to do so; and in fact it did.' This explains why I did what I did, but does it justify it? I do not see that it does.

Davidson goes on to say that non-teleological causal explanations do not display the element of justification provided by reasons. From this, 'some philosophers have concluded that the concept of cause that applies elsewhere cannot apply to the relation between reasons and actions'.[14] It is perfectly true that a cause explains the effect it causes, but cannot justify it. 'Suppose', Davidson says, 'that we grant that reasons alone justify actions in the course of explaining them.'[15] I agree that, in some cases, they can. What Davidson goes on to say from this point onwards strikes me, however, as unnecessarily complicated, and I find it very difficult to make sense of it.[16] But let me try.

I start from what Davidson has asked us to take for granted. It does not follow, he says, that the explanation of an action is not also, and necessarily, causal. He adds: 'if rationalization is, as I want to argue, a species of causal explanation, then justification [in the anaemic sense] is at least one differentiating property'.[17] We are still in the realm of reasons and causes, but dealing with a special kind of cause. A bit further along, Davidson writes, 'the agent performed the action *because* he had the reason', emphasizing the 'because'. He says that we have to 'account for the force of that "because"'.[18] The reason why the agent did what he did, he says, makes the action intelligible.[19] On this account, the familiar picture which it fits the action into, includes 'some of the agent's beliefs and attitudes; perhaps also goals, ends, principles, general character traits, virtues or vices'.[20] What we thus come to see, Davidson says, is 'the point of the action in its setting of rules, practices, conventions, and expectations'.[21] I am still waiting, with bated breath, where this is going to take us in connection with Davidson's claim that 'reasons are causes'. He continues:

> First, we can't infer, from the fact that giving reasons merely rede-scribes the action ['Why are you bobbing around that way?'– 'I'm knitting'] and that causes are separate from effects, that therefore reasons are not causes. Reasons, being beliefs and attitudes, are certainly not identical with actions; but, more important, events are often redescribed in terms of their causes . . . Second, it is an error to think that because placing the action in a larger pattern explains it, therefore, we now understand the sort of explanation involved. Talk of patterns and contexts does not answer the question of how reasons explain actions, since the relevant pattern or context contains both reason and action.[22]

I should simply like to put a marker here, and will return to this question in the second part of my discussion. For now, I will merely note that Davidson answers the objection at an extremely superficial level, and that the question whether or not reasons are causes still remains open.

Davidson next turns to an example used by A. I. Melden in his book *Free Action*: a driver raises his arm to signal a right turn. Davidson asks: What is the pattern that explains the action? Well, he is driving a car in traffic, with other cars on the road, rules that regulate traffic, etc., all of this belonging to a particular form of life in which the participants interact, communicate, and so on. The pattern in question is the sequence of actions within this whole situation. The very pattern, its identity, cannot be divorced from all this; it is only against this background that the pattern is what it is. However, Davidson is not satisfied: 'This explanation does not touch the question of why he raised his arm'. Doesn't it? The driver wanted to make a right turn and avoid the risk of an accident with oncoming traffic. Davidson protests: 'If the description "signalling" explains his action by giving his reason, then the signalling must be intentional; but, on the account just given, it may not be'.[23] The driver may not have thought 'I had better etc.', he may not have formulated an intention before sticking his arm out the window; but that does not mean that his action was not intentional. His intention was in his action.

Davidson persists:

> If, as Melden claims, causal explanations are 'wholly irrelevant to the understanding we seek of human action' then we are without an analysis of the 'because' in 'He did it because . . .', where we go on to name a reason . . . He did it *because* he was driving in traffic, he was approaching a cross road and wanted to turn right.[24]

Is it not obvious that in the situation I have just described this was the driver's reason, and that his reason is the 'because'? If Davidson finds the connection mysterious – which, being a philosopher, it is his privilege to do, even if he ends up alienating himself from the familiar, he can remove the mystery by returning from his philosophical exile to the familiar situation in which this connection can be found. The connection is *embedded in* that situation. Here, Davidson returns to what he calls a 'pro attitude'. Fine, but so far I still cannot detect any progress towards 'reasons as causes'. We now come to section IV of Davidson's paper, which begins as follows:

> In order to turn the first 'and' to 'because' in 'He exercised *and* he wanted to reduce and thought exercise would do it', we must, as the basic move, augment condition C_1 with: C_2. A primary reason for an action is its cause.[25]

C_1 was mentioned earlier in the section, and reads:

> R is a primary reason why an agent performed the action A under the description *d* only if R consists of a pro attitude of the agent toward actions with a certain property, and a belief of the agent that A, under description d, has that property.[26]

(I must say, if this was the only way to do philosophy, I would have given it up long ago. But now I proceed, grinding my teeth.)

The considerations in favour of C_2 may be obvious to Davidson; they are far from obvious to me. If Davidson thinks otherwise, this is because, for him, the 'because' here signifies a cause. But does it? Must it do so? These are questions to which I will return.

Davidson considers as an objection to his position the following claim: 'Primary reasons consist of attitudes and beliefs, which are states or dispositions, not events; therefore they cannot be causes'.[27] He replies that 'states, dispositions, and conditions are frequently named as the causes of events'. He gives an example: the bridge collapsed because of a structural defect. Davidson rightly comments: 'Mention of a causal condition for an event gives a cause only on the assumption that there was also a preceding event'.[28] For instance, a heavy lorry tried to cross the river. The bridge would have supported it, had it not had a structural defect. Davidson raises the question of how this would work in the case of an action. For example, 'a desire to hurt your feeling may spring up at the moment you anger me.' Presumably my disposition to hurt you is unfriendly, or I lack self-control. Davidson writes: 'Those who have argued that there are no mental events to qualify as causes of actions have often missed the obvious because they have insisted that a mental event be observed or noticed (rather than on observing or noticing) . . .'[29] He then turns to Melden's example:

> To dignify a driver's awareness that his turn has come by calling it an experience, or even a feeling, is no doubt exaggerated, but whether it deserves a name or not, it had better be the reason why he raises his arm.[30]

All right. But what makes Davidson think that it is, at the same time, a cause? He writes:

> The signalling driver can answer the question, 'Why did you raise your arm when you did?', and from the answer we learn the event that caused the action . . . Sometimes the answer will mention a mental event that does not give a reason: 'Finally I made up my mind.' However, there also seem to be cases of intentional action where we cannot explain at all why we acted when we did. In such cases, explanation in terms of primary reasons parallels the explanation in terms of the collapse of the bridge from a structural defect: we are ignorant of the event or sequence of events that led up to (caused) the collapse, but we are sure there was such an event or sequence of events.[31]

I will simply comment that the parallel or similarity is a superficial one – a similarity of form, applied to radically different circumstances with radically different grammars. Let me go back to the beginning of the passage I have just quoted: '"Why did you raise your arm when you did?", and from the answer we learn the event that caused the action.' Who says that this is what we learn, and on what basis? Compare and contrast 'As I was driving, I suddenly came to a crossroads covered in bright lights which caused me to blink' with 'I suddenly came to a crossroads where I had to turn right; I immediately signalled a right turn'. In the first instance, it is *my eyes* that are caused to blink; as in the case of the knee jerk, I have nothing to do with this. In the second case, the signalling is something *I* do. Well, can I not be caused to do something?

I can be *made* to laugh: 'The funny story *made* me laugh.' But laughing is different from blinking: I have to understand the joke, and must have a sense of humour. Here, the verb 'to make' is a causal one but only in its 'surface grammar'. Is laughing here, then, something I do, or is it something that happens to me? I am inclined to say that *neither* side of this dichotomy can quite capture what is at issue. Laughing is not something I do, although it is something I enter into, participate in. I would put it like this: it is thanks to the story that I laughed. I engage with the story. It is not like an acid smell that makes me sneeze.

'You *made* me happy.' It is not as if you waved a magic wand and I became happy, similarly to the way your insult might have made me fly off the handle. Even here, where your insult sparks off my anger, what we have is different from, say, a sudden, loud sound that makes me jump. The anger involves or contains me in a way that my reaction to the sudden sound does not. The latter catches me by surprise; had I not been distracted or 'elsewhere in my thoughts', I would not have been caught unawares. It is in my 'absence' that it makes me jump. The Turkish expression for such a case is 'fos, bulun dum'– 'I was empty of myself, I was not there'.

'You *made* me do it.' There are different possibilities here: you may threaten me, manipulate me, deceive me, or persuade me. But what I do involves my responsibility, insofar as it makes sense for me to assume responsibility for whatever I do in response to your actions.

There is a whole spectrum of cases, and matters are far from clear-cut. However, the main point is that the divide, even if not clear-cut, crosses a difference in 'depth grammar'. In the one case, we have a human being with a gamut of interwoven capacities developed in interactions with others and in situations belonging to a life with others. In the other case, we are dealing with the body of anatomy which one both owns and which is owned by one. Does this mean that there is no such thing as 'psycho-logical causation'? I shall briefly try to answer this question below. Next, Davidson considers Melden's argument that 'a cause must be "logically distinct from the alleged effect"; but a reason for an action is not logically distinct from the action; therefore, reasons are not causes of action'.[32]

I am afraid I find Davidson's treatment of this objection superficial. Let me briefly recapitulate what he says: 'Since a reason makes an action intel-ligible by redescribing it', Davidson argues, 'we do not have two events, but only one under different descriptions. Causal relations, however, demand distinct events.'[33] We can express the relation as one between two distinct events: what caused me to switch on the light was my *wanting* to do so. These two are logically distinct; they have independent existences from each other. This is perfectly true: I can want to switch on the light but still not switch it on. I can also switch on the light at gunpoint, even though I have no desire to switch it on. What Melden says is that causal relations are 'external relations', and that the relation between a desire and what is desired is an 'internal relation': 'The very notion of a causal sequence logically implies that cause and effect are intelligible without any logically internal relation of the one to the other'.[34] Melden's book *Free Action* provides a very detailed and lucid discussion of this question.

Davidson considers various other objections to his claim that our rea-sons are the causes of our actions. As there is a great deal more to cover in this chapter, I shall not consider his replies to all of these but merely take up his response to Melden: 'Melden . . . says that actions are often identical with bodily movements, and that bodily movements have causes; yet he denies that the causes are causes of the actions. This is, I think, a contra-diction'.[35] It is possible that Davidson may have misunderstood Melden. Let me clarify the issue in relation to Melden's example of signalling a right turn in traffic. This involves a bodily movement. If I am to make this bodily movement, certain physiological causes must be operative. If my arm were paralysed, I would not be able to move it and succeed in giving the traffic signal. However, I do not use or activate parts of my body in the way a machinist operates a machine – the arm of a crane, say. Nor do I learn to move my arm or legs that way. Indeed, I learnt – as a child – to move parts of my body, as I learn to perform various actions.

Now, the nervous impulses which cause the arm to move are not intentionally initiated by the agent. Indeed, he knows nothing about them. What he does is put into practice what he has learned to do when signalling a right-hand turn. The nervous impulses automatically come into operation when he gives the right-hand-turn signal; they enable him to do what he does. They are *not* the cause of the action. What Davidson calls the cause of the action is that which makes him give the signal, namely the circumstances, his appreciation of what those circumstances amount to, his judgement in the face of these circumstances, and his putting into practice what he has learned to do in such circumstances. This is *neither* causing the agent's arm to go up, *nor* is it causing the agent to give a right-hand-turn signal. What enables him to move his arm so as to signal a right-hand turn is not something he does; and what he does *not* do is to activate nervous impulses. What he does, and what happens in his body, are two different things, indeed two grammatically different *orders* of things.[36]

Contrary to Davidson, Melden does not say that actions are often identical with bodily movements. This is a form of reductionism which it would be insulting to attribute to Melden. Actions are no more identical with bodily movements than a flag *is* a coloured piece of cloth. Actions involve bodily movements, and in the circumstances which surround them they add up to something categorically different. It is not too difficult to spell out this kind of transformation.

'Why on earth', so Davidson rhetorically asks, 'should a cause turn an action into a mere happening and a person into a helpless victim?'[37] The short answer is that there is a radical, categorical difference between something that happens to me, e.g. a fit or a paroxysm of coughing – something which assails me – and something I do, something for which I can be praised or blamed, something for which I can assume responsibility. I am not necessarily a helpless victim of something that happens to me, but I am at least an observer or a witness of it, in *some* ways like a third person. To stop it, if it is unwelcome, I have to hold down my left hand with my right hand, or take a pill, etc., – something I could ask a third person to help me with.

2. Weakness of Will

I now turn to Davidson's second essay and will try to outline it much more briefly than I did the first one. The first part of the essay is merely descriptive of the issue: What is weakness of will? In one case, we have someone who *lacks* the will-power to do what he knows or believes to be better. In the other, he does what he knows to be wrong; he cannot stop himself, contain himself, even though he would like to.

Davidson quotes various people who have given expression to weakness of will, among them the famous words of St Paul.[38] He distinguishes between momentary weakness and weakness of character, between moral weakness and weakness of will. Davidson comments on the way two different themes are interwoven: (i) where desire distracts us from the good, or forces us to be bad, and (ii) 'incontinent action', where the incontinent man goes against his better judgement. He points out that the incontinent man thus acts and judges irrationally.[39]

According to Davidson, the philosophical problem is this: 'Why would anyone ever perform an action when he thought that, everything considered, another action would be better?', 'What is the agent's reason for doing *a* when he believes it would be better, all things considered, to do another thing?' 'In the case of incontinence', he writes, 'the attempt to read reason into behaviour is necessarily subject to a degree of frustration'.[40]

So, in this paper Davidson tries to arrive at a characterization of weakness of will and then sets out what he sees as the philosophical problem this poses for him. He does not go further than that. This is fair enough.

3. Agency

Clearly, Davidson is here concerned with human agency, with the capacity of human beings to act. He asks: what are a person's deeds and his doings, in contrast to mere happenings in his personal history? What is the mark that distinguishes his actions? 'Many examples', Davidson says, 'can be settled out of hand, and this encourages the hope that there is an interesting principle at work'.[41] He adds: 'Philosophers often seem to think that there must be some simple grammatical litmus of agency; but none have been discovered'.[42] Davidson wonders whether 'being intentional is the relevant distinguishing mark'. He points out, however, that though 'intentional implies agency; the converse does not hold'.[43]

One of his examples is the following: I may intentionally spill the contents of my cup, mistakenly thinking that it is tea when it is coffee. Here, the spilling of the coffee is something I do, but under that description it is not what I intended to do.[44] 'On the other hand', Davidson adds, 'if I spill the coffee because you jiggle my hand, I cannot be called an agent'.[45] He thus distinguishes three different cases in which it is correct to say that I spilled the coffee: (i) I do so intentionally, (ii) I do not do so intentionally, but it is my action, (iii) What is in question is not my action at all.

Next, Davidson considers certain kinds of mistakes: misreading a sign, misinterpreting an order, underestimating a weight, miscalculating a sum. Such mistakes are not intentional, though they are actions. To make them, Davidson explains, is to fail to do what one intends; the mistake is not intentional, but, to stick with the last case, the *calculating* is: 'a miscalculation is a calculation'.[46]

Davidson then asks: can we now say which events involve agency? This unexpected and sudden switch from actions to events leaves me uncomfortable. 'Intentional actions do', he answers, 'and so do some other things we do.'[47] Is an action something that happens? One could, perhaps, speak of someone else's action as an event or happening. One could say that a leader's extraordinary action was an event in the history of a nation. But my own action? It is not something that happens to me; from my perspective, it is not an event. The difference between an action and an event is a logical or categorical one. To ask which events involve agency, or which events are actions, is to confuse them. For Davidson the question is, indeed, a stepping stone to his causal theory of actions. However, I do agree with what he goes on to say next, viz. that 'a man is the agent of an act if what he does can be described under an aspect that makes it intentional'.[48]

Davidson gives the example of Hamlet, who kills the man behind the arras. He intended to kill him. He did not know that this man was Polonius, Ophelia's father. Had he known, he would certainly not have killed him. He did not kill Polonius intentionally. According to Davidson, this does not mean that the same action was both intentional and unintentional. Of course not. Davidson then gives another example, of an officer torpedoing and sinking the *Bismarck* while mistakenly thinking it is the *Tirpitz* and intending to sink the latter. He comments: 'it is clearer now why mistakes are actions, for making a mistake must be doing something with the intention of achieving a result that is not forthcoming'.[49]

All this is true, but where does it get us? I have the impression that we are skating on the surface of our language, clarifying its peculiar characteristics. Davidson's discussion continues accordingly: 'It might be thought that the concept of an action is hopelessly indistinct because it is hard to decide whether or not knocking over a policeman, say, or falling down stairs, etc., is an action'.[50] I agree with much of what he says here, but do not find it particularly exciting.

In the penultimate paragraph of Davidson's essay, the linguistic considerations to which I have drawn attention lead him to conclude that

> the extensionality of the expression of agency suggests that the concept of agency is simpler or more basic than that of intention, but unfortunately the route we have travelled does not show how to exploit the hint . . . We should try to see if we can find a mark of agency that does not use the concept of intention. The notion of cause may provide the clue. With respect to causation there is a certain rough symmetry between intention and agency.[51]

In the example that follows, Davidson speaks of desire – Smith's desire to collect the insurance on his house – as the *cause* of his action, viz. his setting the house on fire.[52] I would argue that this is a mistake. I believe that Melden has argued this both clearly and conclusively. Why did Smith burn the house down? Because he wanted to collect the insurance on it. It is with this aim that he set fire to the house. Wanting is not a mental object or event, and what the agent wanted to do, the object of his desire, is its intentional object, where the relation between the two is an *internal* relation – as opposed to a causal and, therefore, external relation.

We can say that it was the desire to obtain so-and-so that *made* him do it. On the face of it, 'make' is a causal word. Does this mean that my desire was the cause of my action? I certainly caused the fire by lighting a match. What I caused here, was an event. What did my desire cause? Certainly not the fire. If the claim is that my desire caused my action, that it caused me to burn the house down, then what happens to me, the agent? Did the desire cause me to do it? Even if the cause here works through my will, I am a puppet. If it makes me decide to do it, then my decision will be a fake decision: it looks like a decision, but is not one that I take. It is imposed on me, though I am self-deceived and believe that I took it myself. There are such cases, of course, but the one we are considering is not one of them. Indeed, we identify such a case by contrasting it with a genuine case of agency, responsibility, etc.

I repeat: I cause the fire – an event. I do so by what I do – my action. But I do not cause my action. I am not the cause of my action; I am its agent – the person who performs it. How do I do it? By striking a match. How do I strike a match? By moving my fingers, etc. How do I move my fingers? Not by doing something else. I have learned to move my fingers, limbs, etc., in learning to do things. As for my desires, the things I want, these are not mental events with causal powers. When I want something or when I want to do something, I use my judgement and put into practice what I have learned in the course of my growth and development. If my desire was the cause of what I do to fulfil it, it would either pass me by or work through my will, in which case my intention or decision would be fake.

Davidson asks: 'Can we then say that to be the author or agent of an event is to cause it?'[53] My answer is: of course we can, and we do. Davidson says that this is 'ordinary event causality'.[54] Indeed, he goes on: 'Event causality can spread responsibility for an action to the consequences of the action, but it cannot help explicate the first attribution of agency on which the rest depend'.[55] So, event causality cannot explain the relation between an agent and a primitive action. All right, I agree. Perhaps I have jumped the gun.

Further along, Davidson writes: 'It may be true that I cause my finger to move by contracting certain muscles.'[56] Normally, I would say that I move my finger, for instance, to touch something. But it is true that in learning to walk along difficult mountain paths, I learn what muscles to use. Once I have learned the skill, I contract my muscles without thinking: my muscles, then, are not the object of my intentions. Davidson also says: 'Possibly I cause the muscles to contract by making an event occur in my brain.'[57] I would say that I know nothing about my brain; but when I move my finger, it is more than likely that what I do causes some activity in my brain. Either way, Davidson agrees that, in this context, pointing my finger is a primitive action. 'Doing something that causes my finger to move does not cause me to move my finger; it *is* moving my finger'.[58] Yes, except that I do not do something that causes my finger to move. I simply move my finger. This is what Davidson calls 'a primitive action'.

Again, I agree with what Davidson presents as R. Chisholm's view in "Freedom and Action", namely that 'although an agent may be said to make certain cerebral events happen when it is these events that cause his finger to move, making the cerebral events happen cannot be called something he does . . . [These] are not events of which he is the agent'.[59]

Earlier I objected to Davidson's claim that the concept of cause may provide the clue as to how we are to understand human agency – to the idea, in other words, of the agent as the cause of his actions. But I must confess that, *so far*, all that Davidson has given us is 'ordinary event causality'.

He writes: 'Action does require that what the agent does is intentional under some description, and this in turn requires, I think, that what the agent does is known to him under some description'.[60] I agree. Davidson continues: 'A man who raises his arm both intends to do with his body whatever is needed to make his arm go up and knows that he is doing it.'[61] Here I do not follow: What does the man intend to do with his body apart from raising his arm? Surely he just raises it – perhaps to greet someone. I won't bother with Davidson's claim that the agent intentionally and knowingly brings about cerebral events.

Davidson now returns to the question whether the concept of action may be analysed in terms of the concept of causality. He writes:

The ordinary notion of event causality is useful in explaining how agency can spread from primitive actions described in further ways, but it cannot in the same way explain the basic sense of agency. What we must ask, then, is whether there is another kind of causality . . . an appeal to which will help us understand agency. We may call this kind of causality . . . *agent causality*.[62]

Davidson then articulates the following dilemma:

> *Either* the causing by an agent of a primitive action is an event
> discrete from the primitive action, in which case we have problems
> about acts of will or worse, *or* it is not a discrete event, in which case
> there seems to be no difference between saying that someone caused
> a primitive action and saying that he was the agent. To take the first
> horn, suppose that causing a primitive action . . . does introduce an
> event separate and . . . prior to the action. This prior event in turn
> must either be an action, or not. If an action, then the action we began
> with was not . . . primitive. If not an action, then we have tried to
> explain agency by appeal to an even more obscure notion, that of a
> causing that is not a doing.[63]

In the second case, we suppose that agent causation does *not* introduce
an event in addition to the primitive action. But here the concept of *cause*
seems to play no role.[64] Davidson concludes that

> there seems no good reason, therefore, for using such expressions
> as 'cause', 'bring about', 'make the case' to *illuminate* the relation
> between an agent and his act . . . Causality is central to the concept
> of agency, but it is ordinary causality between events that is relevant,
> and it concerns the effects and not the causes of actions.[65]

I am doubtful whether this round trip down the garden path has illumi-
nated anything for me, whether it has taught me anything I did not know.
Davidson now takes up Joel Feinberg's 'accordion effect'. For example,
someone flicks the switch. He thus turns the light on and illuminates the
room. As a consequence, he alerts a prowler. On the one hand, this is a
causal sequence. On the other hand, these are descriptions of what he has
done, whether intentionally or unintentionally. He did not know that there
was a prowler, and so did not alert him intentionally. 'In brief', Davidson
concludes, 'once he has done one thing (move a finger) each consequence
presents us with a deed; an agent causes what his action causes'.[66]

All right. What the agent causes is what his action causes. He causes the
light to come on. This is 'event causality'. But, Davidson would ask, did
we not also say that in flicking the switch he turns the light on? This is a
wider description of his action. Yes, but we have two different descriptions
here: (i) the light comes on, (ii) he turns on the light. What he causes by
his action – flicking the switch – is an event, the light comes on. It is *not*
his action under the wider description (as the bellows of the accordion

expand). I repeat: what the agent causes, his action causes; and that is an event, not an action. The agent does not cause his actions. I mean this as a grammatical remark.

Davidson says that 'the accordion effect is limited to agents'.[67] As I understand it, this means that the causal effects of what a person does can be described as something he did intentionally, in the right circumstances. Thus, not only did Jones strike the ball, he also broke the window. But, Davidson notes, we do not say that the bat with which Jones struck the ball broke the window. He concludes: 'It seems therefore that we may take the accordion effect as a mark of agency'.[68]

The only thing I can make of this convoluted claim is that an agent can come to know himself through acting, can reason about the consequences of his actions and be praised or blamed for these, and assume responsibility. A baseball bat, on the other hand, which can equally cause a window to be broken, cannot be attributed any responsibility for this outcome. Now, there are certainly questions here which call for illumination. Unfortunately, Davidson's philosophical round trip has not provided any.

'The accordion effect', he writes, 'is interesting because it shows that we treat the consequences of actions differently from the way we treat the consequences of other events'.[69] Of course. But – and I apologise for insisting on this – we did not need the accordion to be told of this. Davidson's next sentence reads: 'This suggests that there is, after all, a fairly simple linguistic test that sometimes reveals that we take an event to be an action'.[70] My response is to ask, Do we need such a test? What for? Surely, we know how to recognize a human action. Surely, what we want and seek as philosophers is to understand what it is that makes a human action an action, how it involves the responsibility of the person whose action it is, etc. A linguistic test, if it existed, would not provide us with that understanding. In any case, Davidson cannot find such a test or criterion; he abandons the search and turns 'to a related question that has come to the fore in [his] discussion of agent causality and the accordion effect'.[71]

Davidson says that his new question concerns the relation between an agent and those of his actions that are not primitive, viz. actions he has wrought 'in the world beyond his skin'. He writes: 'Assuming that we understand agency in the case of primitive actions, how exactly are such actions related to the rest?'[72] It seems to me that Davidson's assumptions about what philosophers understand about these matters needs discussion. Melden, in his book *Free Action*, does devote a great deal of space to the discussion of such 'primitive' actions, as Davidson calls them. As far as the latter's new question goes, his discussion covers the six or so pages of his essay. Here, all the fuss evaporates, and I do not disagree with what Davidson says, except that I find nothing controversial or exciting in it:

1   What is involved in 'the accordion effect of agency' is effect agency.
2   It is a mistake to think that when I close the door of my own free will anyone normally causes me to do it. Primitive actions are those we do not do by doing something else. (But this needs much further discussion.)
3   When I close the door by moving my hand I do not perform two numerically distinct actions. ('Primitive actions [are] mere movements of the body – these are all the actions there are. We never do more than move our bodies: the rest is up to nature')[73]
4   'The relation between an agent and his action – [here] the notion of cause has nothing directly to do with this relation . . . Causality allows us to redescribe actions in ways in which we cannot redescribe other events; this fact is a mark of actions, but yields no analysis of agency'.[74]

Just a few pages into the essay, Davidson writes: 'We should try to see if we can find a mark of agency that does not use the concept of intention. The notion of cause may provide the clue'.[75] Fairly soon after, this hope collapses: '. . . I abandon the search for an analysis of the concept of agency that does not appeal to intention'.[76] The essay is an honest one, but I have not found it easy to summarize. I hope to return to some of the questions Davidson raises in this and the other essays, and to make my own contribution to their clarification.

4.   Freedom to Act
There are philosophers who believe that freedom is inconsistent with the assumption that actions are causally determined. Davidson notes that he will not be concerned with this view, since it has been widely discussed by others. 'The other attack [on the claim that free actions are caused by desires, beliefs, etc.] is more interesting', he says:

> It is aimed not at determinism as such, but at the causal theory of action. If a free action is one that is caused in certain ways, then freedom to act must be a *causal power* of the action that comes into play when certain conditions are satisfied.[77]

Thus, we are back with the causal theory of action. Davidson begins with an attempt to clarify what it would mean to say that freedom to act is a *causal power* of the action that comes into play when certain conditions are satisfied. If I may jump the gun, this suggests to me that a person is free to do something if he has the capacity to do it or chooses to do it. Davidson's analysis makes heavy weather of this. As he puts it: 'It is natural to say that a person can do something (or is free to do it) if all that is required, if he is to do it, is that he *will* to do it'.[78] Fair enough. Here, 'will to do it' must mean 'choose to do it'. Davidson asks whether 'he would do it if he were to will to do it' expresses a causal disposition. Later on, he compares that causal disposition to a self-sealing tank, but this strikes me as a diversion, as carefulness gone crazy.[79] Either way, Davidson now sets out a dilemma: (a) If willing is an act distinct from doing it, it might be a cause. But then, when is an agent free to will? (b) If willing is not an act distinct from doing, then it cannot be a case of the doing. Davidson asks: If the dilemma cannot be resolved, shouldn't we abandon the causal theory of action?

Again, let me intervene at the cost – as it would seem to Davidson – of simplifying. A person may have the capacity to do something or to bring about a state of affairs. For the moment, I make no distinction. I would not dignify this by calling it 'a causal power' – it is a mouthful. Surely, the question is whether the agent exercises the capacity freely, chooses freely: is his choice causally determined, or is it not? If it is causally determined, then it is not *he* that chooses, though it may seem to him that he does. If, on the other hand, it is *he* who makes the choice – and what this involves needs discussion – then he chooses and acts freely. I would say that sometimes the former is the case, sometimes the latter. And if it can be the case that the agent's choice is causally determined when it *seems* to him that he chooses freely (i.e. when he is self-deceived), then it must be possible for him to choose freely *in reality*. But let me return to Davidson.

He believes that the above dilemma can be resolved and many of the objections to a causal analysis of freedom circumvented. He says that he will argue for this view. But the fuss he makes about arriving at an analysis of 'causal power' is beyond me. What could it mean to say that *a person* has a causal power, except that he has the capacity to do or bring about? Davidson points out that there is little difference between 'The heat caused the flower to wilt' and 'The heat caused the wilting of the flower'. By contrast, he says, there can be a great difference between 'The heat caused Samantha to return to Patna' and 'The heat caused Samantha's return to Patna'. I see why Davidson says this, but I think he is wrong. He argues that the former implies, or strongly suggests, a limitation on Samantha's freedom of action. I ask: How did the heat cause her return? It did not light a fuse under her which then propelled her to Patna. No, she found the heat too much and, though she would have liked to stay where she was, she returned to Patna. She could not bear the heat. She was forced, but still she acted freely. There is, of course, a difference between acting freely and not acting freely, but you cannot capture it in this way.

'An *action* may be caused without the *agent* being caused to perform it'.[80] Let me think of an example. Suppose that there is someone who, in certain circumstances, upsets and alienates people whom he needs to get along with. He has an appointment with someone whose assistance he needs on an important business matter. He meets him, the conversation goes a certain way, he ends up by upsetting and alienating the other person and, much to his chagrin, he returns from the meeting empty-handed and frustrated. This doesn't quite fit Davidson's description, for the action is caused here through the agent's being caused to perform it.

How can the action be causal without the agent being caused to perform it? Even if he were caused to do something while sleepwalking, it would be through the other person's agency. If, on the other hand, you were to attach electrodes to his brain which caused his arm to go up and knock down a vase, what would be caused in such a case would be a bodily movement and not an action.

Davidson gives the following example: 'Desire caused him to do it'. He says it suggests a lack of control and 'makes the act less than voluntary'. By contrast, the statement 'Desire was the cause of his doing it' leaves the question of freedom open.[81] Normally, if we say that it was because he wanted to go to Africa for so long that he finally did go, the 'because' here is not the because of causation. Indeed, a desire is not a mental event which causes an action. This is a 'grammatical' remark. Where a person *gives in* to an overwhelming desire, it is again *the person* who does so. Suppose the desire were to cloud his judgement. We would then say that he acted with a clouded judgement. Even when – to take an extreme case – a sleepwalker does something, what he does is an action. I will not comment on his responsibility. As for 'desire was the cause of his doing it', which I would rephrase as, 'he did it because he desired . . .' – yes, of course, it leaves the question of his freedom open, indeed more than open; on the face of it, there is no suggestion that he acted unfreely. I think we are now rehearsing what I regard as platitudes.

The next few pages of Davidson's paper are about G. E. Moore and Austin's 'If and cans', which I have discussed elsewhere;[82] I shall therefore ignore them here, also because they are written in an abstract style, which puts me off. Davidson then continues:

> We have now decided on a two-part theory of what a man can do; one part aims to explain what he can do intentionally, and the other

part extends this to what the intentional would cause . . . To say a man can do x intentionally is to say he would do it if – what?[83]

I find it difficult to understand and follow Davidson's language here. I suppose that a man can do something accidentally, something he could not have intended to do because he never learnt it and so wouldn't know how to do it. All right, so when he does it accidentally, he causes something to happen. For example, he brings two wires together and causes an explosion which destroys a building. He destroys a building – an action – but accidentally. If you had asked him to destroy or blow up the building, he would have replied, 'I wouldn't know how to do it.' Davidson says: 'In order to be eligible as a cause, the event mentioned must be separate from the action; but if it is separate from the action, there is . . . always the possibility of asking about *it*, whether the agent is free to do it.'[84] If he doesn't know how to do it, how can he be free to do it?

Davidson continues: 'The objection applies to choosing, willing, intending and trying. None of these is plausibly the cause of an action.' I agree. 'Sometimes, 'choosing or willing to do something are mental acts performed prior to doing the things but in these cases the question does not arise whether the agent is free to do them'.[85] Yes, all right. Davidson concludes that the analysis fails. He writes: 'The only hope for a causal analysis is to find states or events which are causal conditions of intentional actions.'[86] I do not understand what 'causal conditions of intentional actions' means. Davidson goes on: 'The most eligible such states or events are the beliefs and desires of an agent that *rationalize* an action'.[87] Again, I do not understand how beliefs and desires can be causal conditions. Davidson gives a rather bizarre example. A man saws his piano in half, in 'order to throw it out of the window'. Davidson says that obviously this man's reasons or beliefs and desires explain why he acted as he did. Yes, they do. 'We can see', he says, 'that the intention with which he sawed the piano in half was to get the piano out of the window.'[88] Obviously. Next, Davidson formulates an abstract statement: 'A can do x intentionally (under the description *d*) means that if A has desires and beliefs that rationalize x (under d), then A does *x*.'[89] All right.

Davidson concludes: 'A number of previous problems seem to be solved by this analysis. The antecedent condition is prior to and separate from the action, and so is suited to be a course.'[90] This looks to me like playing with a causal theory of action as if it were a yo-yo: one moment it is up, the next one it is down. This, too, is not an objection. I have already said that desires, beliefs and reasons are not causes of actions. Davidson asks: What about coming to have desires and beliefs that constitute reasons for actions? 'Coming to have them', he says, 'is not something an agent does.'[91] Again, I cannot agree. Desires and beliefs are not visitations from outer space; a person comes to have them in different ways. They are what a person can own, make his own. He bears a responsibility for them, whether he is prepared to shoulder it or not.

After several long paragraphs of abstract reasoning, Davidson concludes: 'If . . . rationalizing attitudes do cause an action of mine, then not only does the action occur, but it is, under the rationalized description, intentional'.[92] Did it require such somersaults to find this out? Davidson adds: 'This is, of course, what we should expect: what an agent does do intentionally is what he is free to do *and* has adequate reasons for doing'.[93] This is a platitude, though I have to add a qualification below.

Davidson next points out that many philosophers maintain 'that an action is freely performed only if the agent was, when he did it, free to abstain: he could have done otherwise' – i.e. he had no choice but to do it. He continues: 'If the causal theory derives us to this, why isn't the libertarian right when he denies that freedom can be reconciled with the causal theory?'[94] Davidson goes on: 'Two intuitions seem at war, and the territory that is threatened with destruction is occupied by the causal theory . . . The puzzle is resolved by [the] discovery that what depends on the agent is the intentional performance of an act of a certain sort.'[95] True, indeed. So, why cling to the causal theory? 'It is true', Davidson argues, 'that it may sometimes be the case that what a man does intentionally he might have been caused to do anyway, by alien forces.'[96] I agree, but I would express this differently. In my writings on moral philosophy, I have drawn a distinction between a 'determining psychology' and an 'enabling psychology', and shall return to this. The 'alien forces' which, according to Davidson, function as 'causes', are dissociated parts of the agent. The agent's freedom, I have argued, is to be gained by 'inner work' directed towards owning these dissociated parts of the person, in the course of which he is transformed and comes to himself, as it were. But, so Davidson goes on, 'what a man does intentionally he might have been caused [driven] to do anyway', in which case what he does is not intentional.[97]

I agree, albeit with a qualification. Take an example: Someone goes out of his way to say something hurtful to his friend, which he believes he is saying for the latter's own good. In reality, he says it out of hostility, to get his own back on his friend for a real or imaginary offence which he resents. His intention to tell his friend something that will be for the latter's benefit is bogus. His (apparent) action is not intentional in that sense. What he is doing, even though he doesn't recognize it, is very different from the way it appears to him in his self-deception. In truth, he is doing something very different; he intends to hurt his friend, to pay him back for a real or imaginary offence. That action, the one he doesn't own, is intentional; but the intention is unconscious. An unconscious intention belongs to what I call a 'determining psychology'. Here the person does not act freely.[98] Let me note, in passing, that even here I prefer not to talk of a cause. For it is the person himself who stands in his way or drives himself in a direction he does not recognize or acknowledge. As Davidson puts it: 'what he does, in the broader sense, may occur whether or not he wills it'.[99] I would prefer to say: whether or not he consciously intends it.

I will not consider the final pages of Davidson's 'Freedom to Act'. He still harks back to the causal theory and notes towards the end of his essay that 'we must count our search for a causal analysis of "A is free to do x" a failure'.[100] Yet his last words are: '. . . there is no obstacle to the view that freedom to act is a causal power of the agent'.[101] If by 'the causal power of an agent' is meant his capacity to do things and to bring things about by means of what he does – and hence by his capacity to act intentionally – then yes, an intentional agent *can* act freely. But what a way to reach this conclusion!

To be fair, in both this and the other essays I have examined, Davidson works hard and honestly. He is clearly a very intelligent man and a sophisticated philosopher, sometimes too intelligent for me (I say this in all modesty). But I find his writing, at least in these essays, sprawling. That is why I find him difficult to summarize. I also find his intellectualism to be lacking in depth, and his facility in abstract reasoning a liability rather than an asset. His way of doing philosophy, though by no means alien to me, is – if I may put it colloquially –'not my cup of tea'. I would much rather read Melden's book *Free Action*.

5.   Intending

This essay starts with some perfectly true, not to say platitudinous, remarks about the concept of intention. One can form an intention, but one may not execute it. One may have an intention, but not form it through practical reasoning. Davidson calls this a 'pure intention'. Someone who acts with an intention, acts for a reason; he has something in mind that he wants to accomplish. Let me add: one can act intentionally without forming an intention – e.g. I open the door and walk out of the room. My action is intentional, but I have not gone through any reasoning or decision. Actually, Davidson has this on his list of intentional actions as well.[102] He goes on to formulate a general statement of what it is to act with an intention, but the formulation is too long to quote here. Davidson then resuscitates the ghost of causation, laid to rest so many times in the previous essays: 'An action is performed with a certain intention if it is caused in the right way by attitudes and beliefs that rationalize it.'[103]

Davidson adds another remark: 'Acting with an intention does not require that there be any mysterious act of will or special attitude or episode of willing'.[104] I agree. He says that this 'reduction is not definitional but ontological'.[105] All right. Davidson elaborates that this 'ontological reduction . . . is enough to answer many puzzles about the relation between the mind and the body and to explain the possibility of autonomous action in a world of causality'.[106]

This is intimately connected with the way Wittgenstein contrasts, say, a bout of anger with an intention. An intention, Wittgenstein notes, does not have 'genuine duration'.[107] One can pay attention to the sound of a siren or a bout of anger. One can tell when it changes and determine how long it lasts by a stop-watch. What has 'genuine duration' is something that goes on. By contrast, 'I had the intention of . . .' does not express the memory of an experience (any more than 'I was on the point of . . .' does). Intending is not a state of consciousness. It does not have genuine duration. Someone says: 'I have the intention of going away tomorrow.' Wittgenstein asks: 'When have you that intention? The whole time or intermittently?' These questions are meant to bring out the absurdity of the idea of an intention as a mental process. For a process is something that has 'genuine duration'.[108]

When Davidson speaks of this as an 'ontological reduction', he means that an intention is not the object of an 'inner experience'. As Wittgenstein would say, when one tries to remember a past intention or the intention with which one did something, one does not try to remember some particular thing, an inner object or experience which is the intention: 'One remembers thoughts, feelings, movements, and also connections with earlier situations. It is as if one had altered the adjustment of a microscope. One did not see before what is now in focus'.[109] Davidson says that this 'reduction' helps to answer many puzzles regarding the relation between the mind and the body. I agree. To my mind, however, Davidson does not show us how – at any rate not to my satisfaction. (At the end of this chapter, I shall explain my misgivings in an extended quote from *Love and Human Separateness*.)

At this point, Davidson turns to what he calls 'pure intending'. 'Often', he says, 'intentional action is not preceded by an intention'.[110] True. He goes on: 'It seems that in an intentional action that takes much time, or involves preparatory steps, something like pure intending must be present'.[111] I find this way of putting it strange: 'something like pure intending must be present'. I open the door to go out. My action is intentional. But

it is not preceded by the formation of an intention. My intention is *in* my action; it does not exist separately from it. Davidson says that in such a case it is likely that the agent's intention is 'a state, disposition, or attitude of some sort'.[112] Is he not harking back here to the Cartesian position which he rejected with his 'ontological reduction'? What he goes on to say next, viz. that 'pure intending merely shows that there is something there to be abstracted', seems to me to confirm the suspicion. In Chapter 5, I shall try to explain the sense in which an intention, in such a case, is *in* the action.

I think that Davidson prolongs this unresolved conflict when he asks whether a pure intention is a state of the agent, and what sort of state it is.[113] Next, he tries a different approach: '*Saying* that one intends to do something . . . is undeniably an action'.[114] The utterance 'forms' an intention and so 'commits the person to doing it'. I agree that 'actually to identify saying one intends to do something with forming an intention' would be 'to endorse a sort of performative theory of intention'.[115] But let me add, *by way of analogy*, that someone – e.g. a farmer planting potatoes or sowing seeds – found digging is committing himself to a pattern of behaviour which he has learnt. It is in just this way that the intention is *in* the action, which is such a pattern unfolding in time. Of course, the agent may change his mind. Or, again, it may be the case that he meant, intended all along, to follow a different pattern. When he does, we realize that either we were mistaken about his intention, about what he was doing, or that he has changed his mind, or – in a third case – that he has broken down, gone out of his mind.

There is little in the closing pages of Davidson's essay that I wish to comment on. Once again, I am afraid that, even though I agree with much of what he says here, I do not find the essay as a whole particularly exciting. I do not say this unkindly, but it is true. Again, I cannot guarantee that the fault is not mine.

What follows is an extended quotation from the second chapter of my book *Love and Human Separateness*, entitled 'Descartes and the Interaction between Mind and Body':

> An intention can, of course, be an object of introspection in the ordinary sense in which when one is unclear about one's intentions one may reflect on one's actions, words, thoughts, past behaviour and present circumstances in order to become clear. Here introspection is self-reflection, not a form of observation by means of a supposed inner sense.
>
> A man's will, as it may find expression in his intention or resolution, is something which only an observer, another person, can see

from the outside, as when he sees the agent bent on carrying out a scheme. It is not something which the person himself sees from the inside. When he tells you what his intentions are he does so without observing anything. That is, he has a way of telling you this which no one else can have without being him. If one puts this by saying that he knows what his intentions are 'from inside' then this is only another way of saying that he knows what he intends to do as only an agent knows this, namely by virtue of having made up his mind.

An intention, then, is not an occurrence in the mind such that we can say, 'Here is the mental, inner component of an action, and there is the physical, outer component, namely the bodily movement'. This is the dualist conception in which the mind and the body are conceptually dissociated from each other.

It is true, of course, that an intention can precede an action and also remain unexecuted. But when the action is carried out the intention is *in* the action. In other words, the two are *internally* related. How? To see this let us think of an action the description of which involves reference to the agent's intention; for instance, a farmer planting potatoes. He could be said to be doing what we see him to be doing, namely putting seed potatoes in the ground, with the intention of growing potatoes. But what is it for the farmer to have such an intention?

To answer this question we have to turn our attention from a supposed inner act to the outer practice – the practice of farming, the knowledge of crops and methods of growing them, and the agent's familiarity with the practice. When, on the basis of what we see him doing, we describe the farmer as planting potatoes, we take it for granted that he knows about crops and how to grow them, and we anticipate what he will go on to do. How he will go on with what he is doing now, given the particular circumstances I have mentioned: this is what is crucial in our characterization of his action as 'planting potatoes'. This is what a reference to his intention brings into focus. It is, of course, important to emphasize that *his* relation to this, namely how he will go on, is different from *our* relation to it.

To see the point in question we need to consider a case where the agent goes on differently from what we anticipate. Perhaps he digs the potatoes out the next day, then he digs them in and he digs them out again. (I am indebted to Rush Rhees for this example.) Would we not now say that though at first we thought that he was planting potatoes, intending to grow them, we must have been mistaken. Of course, we have to allow for the possibility of half-executed intentions, such as when the agent changes his mind, loses interest in what he is doing or abandons his project half way through. But it remains true that unexecuted and half-executed intentions make sense only in relation to fully executed ones; that is, to the completed action which constitutes the fulfilment of the intention. For it is this which he envisages carrying out; the intention has the completed pattern as its object. To have it the agent must have a grasp of his pattern and it is his practical knowledge that gives him this grasp. He utilizes it in executing the intention. He does not, like the observer, predict that what he will go on to do will conform to the pattern in question; he conforms to it in what he does.

So a person acquires a will – and that means the capacity to make decisions; from resolutions, act with intention – in learning to act. At first when the child does something at will the intention lies *in* the action, it has no existence apart from the action. Here the action is *constitutive* of the intention. The intention acquires a separate existence only after the child learns to consider whether or not to do certain things in particular situations, when he is able to think about future situations or future developments of his present situation which may call for certain actions now. It is in this way that he becomes capable of having intentions which he may not execute and which therefore precede his actions. But, to repeat, it does so only where a man knows how to perform the action. It still presupposes the existence of the pattern to be realized and the agent's practical knowledge. It can exist apart from the action, this is only because originally it resides in the action. Here too the relation between the intention and the action which fulfils it, whether or not the agent in fact executes, is internal. It cannot be identified without reference to the action, it is not something that has come to be joined to the action which fulfils it.[116]

Notes

1 Donald Davidson, *Essays on Actions and Events* (Oxford: Clarendon Press, 1980), xi.
2 Ibid.
3 Ibid., 3
4 Ibid., 3–4.
5 Ibid., 4.
6 Ibid.
7 Ibid.
8 Ibid., 6.

9 Ibid., 7.
10 Ibid., 7–8.
11 Ibid., 8.
12 Ibid.
13 Ibid., 9.
14 Ibid.
15 Ibid.
16 Ibid.
17 Ibid.
18 Ibid.
19 Ibid., 10.
20 Ibid.
21 Ibid.
22 Ibid.
23 Ibid., 11.
24 Ibid.
25 Ibid., 12.
26 Ibid., 5.
27 Ibid., 12.
28 Ibid.
29 Ibid., 12.
30 Ibid., 13.
31 Ibid.
32 Ibid.
33 Ibid.
34 See A. I. Melden, *Free Action* (London: Routledge & Kegan Paul, 1961), 52.
35 Davidson, *Essays on Actions and Events*, 18–19.
36 Editorial Note: Following Wittgenstein, Dilman here uses the word 'grammatically' to mean 'conceptually'.
37 Davidson, *Essays on Actions and Events*, 19.
38 Ibid., 27–8. 'The good which I want to do, I fail to do; but what I do is the wrong which is against my will; and if what I do is against my will, clearly it is no longer I who am the agent' St Paul, Romans 7.
39 Davidson, *Essays on Actions and Events*, 41.
40 Ibid., 42.
41 Ibid., 43.
42 Ibid., 44.
43 Ibid., 45.
44 Ibid.
45 Ibid.

46 Ibid.
47 Ibid.
48 Ibid., 46.
49 Ibid.
50 Ibid., 47.
51 Ibid.
52 'If I say that Smith set the house on fire in order to collect the insurance, I explain his action, in part, by giving one of its causes, namely his desire to collect the insurance', Ibid., 47.
53 Ibid., 48.
54 Ibid., 49.
55 Ibid.
56 Ibid.
57 Ibid.
58 Ibid., 50.
59 Ibid., 50. See R. Chisholm, 'Freedom and Action', in *Freedom and Determinism*, ed. Keith Lehrer (New York: Random House, 1966), 28–44.
60 Davidson, *Essays on Actions and Events*, 50.
61 Ibid.
62 Ibid., 52.
63 Ibid. My emphasis.
64 Ibid.
65 Ibid., 53.
66 Ibid.
67 Ibid., 54.
68 Ibid.
69 Ibid., 54–5.
70 Ibid., 55.
71 Ibid.
72 Ibid.
73 Ibid., 59.
74 Ibid., 60.
75 Ibid., 47.
76 Ibid., 55.
77 Ibid., 63.
78 Ibid.
79 'Another kind of causal power is such that an object that possesses it is caused to change in a certain way if a prior change takes place in the object. An example might be the property of a tank that is self-sealing. If the tank starts to leak, this causes the leak to seal . . . If freedom to act is a causal power, it belongs to this category.' Ibid., 65.

80 Ibid.
81 Ibid.
82 See my book *Free Will* (London: Routledge, 1999), Chapter 14, 'G. E. Moore: Free Will and Causality', 221–34.
83 Davidson, *Essays on Actions and Events*, 72.
84 Ibid.
85 Ibid.
86 Ibid.
87 Ibid.
88 Ibid., 73.
89 Ibid.
90 Ibid.
91 Ibid.
92 Ibid., 74.
93 Ibid.
94 Ibid.
95 Ibid.
96 Ibid.
97 Ibid., 75.
98 See Ilham Dilman, 'Intentions and the Unconscious', in *Mind, Psycho-Analysis and Science*, ed. Crispin Wright and Peter Clark (Oxford: Blackwell, 1988), 169–87; and Ilham Dilman, *Raskolnikov's Rebirth: Psychology and the Understanding of Good and Evil* (Chicago, Ill.: Open Court, 2000).
99 Davidson, *Essays on Actions and Events*, 75.
100 Ibid., 80.
101 Ibid., 81.
102 Ibid., 85.
103 Ibid., 87.
104 Ibid.
105 Ibid., 88.
106 Ibid.
107 Ludwig Wittgenstein, *Philosophical Investigations*, trans. G. E. M. Anscombe (Oxford: Blackwell, 1999), §§ 81–2.
108 For a discussion of this, see Ilham Dilman, *Love and Human Separateness* (Oxford: Blackwell, 1987), Chapter 2, §4, especially pp. 14–15.
109 Wittgenstein, *Philosophical Investigations*, §645.
110 Davidson, *Essays on Actions and Events*, 88.
111 Ibid.
112 Ibid.
113 Ibid., 89.

114 Ibid., 90.
115 Ibid.
116 Dilman, *Love and Human Separateness*, 15–17.

5 Donald Davidson II: A Philosophy of Psychology, the Mental and the Physical

In this chapter, I wish to consider some of the essays from the final part of Davidson's book, entitled 'Philosophy of Psychology'.

1. Mental Events

Davidson refers to 'perceivings, rememberings, decisions' as 'mental events'.[1] Being a philosopher, it is 'normal' for him to do so; his whole training leads him to speak in this way. In everyday conversation, such talk is innocuous. But behind this way of speaking may lurk Cartesian dualism. We may say to someone who keeps making blunders or who seems to be distracted, 'Where is your mind?' Similarly, we may ask someone who acts stupidly to 'use his mind'. Clearly, we associate thinking with the mind, and thinking is a capacity. It is a capacity of the person, a flesh-and-blood being. There are further capacities with which thinking is tied up, such as remembering, intending, deciding, feeling, knowing, etc. Thus, we can say that the mind is a network of interrelated capacities. As I said above, these are capacities of a flesh-and-blood being, which develops and exercises these in its interactions with others, in a life lived with language. The kind of life in question and the significances embodied in the situations that are characteristic of it, are absolutely essential to the very identity of the capacities thus exercised, as indeed they are to the identity of the flesh-and-blood beings as human beings.

This is why I find the characterization of perceivings, rememberings, etc., as 'mental events' philosophically unhelpful, even when they are innocuous. Be that as it may, Davidson says that these 'mental events . . . resist capture in the nomological net of physical theory'.[2] I am not surprised one bit. Davidson wonders: 'How can this fact be reconciled with the causal role of mental events in the physical world?'[3] I ask: what causal role? I don't know for certain what Davidson has in mind. Perhaps he thinks: I decide to squash a fly that is bothering me – a mental event. So I wave my arm – a physical event. The one causes the other. Thus, a mental event has played a causal role in the physical world, to which my arm and its movement belong. I am not saying that this reading is accurate, but *if* this is what Davidson thinks, then it is crude, Cartesian thinking.

My teacher John Wisdom once asked whether the words 'He is walking very fast' describe 'a purely bodily performance' and whether, by contrast, the words 'He is thinking about the trade cycle' describe 'a purely mental performance'. His response: 'Aren't both both?'[4] Wisdom's point was that thinking is not the initiation of special events to which only the thinker is privy, a process visible only to his inner gaze. Nor, on the other hand, is walking the same as being propelled, or propelling oneself, by certain movements of the legs. Nor is it such propulsion *plus* something else, something going on in the privacy of the person's mind.

One learns to think as one learns to talk and act, all three in harness. Thinking originally belongs with acting, it is implicit in the judgements that find expression in our responses to the situations we face. If thinking can assume an existence that is independent of such responses, we must not forget that its intelligibility is still rooted in the life and language we share with others. Besides, one can easily do on paper what one can do in one's head. What makes either of these activities *thinking* is the role it plays in what I say and what I go on to do. If one remembers this, one will be less inclined to describe thinking as a 'purely mental performance'.

To say, quite rightly, that 'thinking is something mental' is not to say that it is a process that goes on in the mind, namely a sequence of mental events conceived – in Wisdom's words – as a 'private shadow show'. When we speak of thought as 'something mental', we are referring neither to a special medium in which it goes on, nor to any special stuff which constitutes it. We mean that it is the exercise of a 'mental capacity' as opposed to a physical one, in the sense of belonging to the body in a common-or-garden sense. In other words, it is an intellectual capacity and not one that involves, for instance, the muscles. But that which has this capacity is the person, not something in him called 'the mind'.

Similarly for an activity like walking, which is something I do 'with intention', e.g. when I take exercise or set out to go somewhere by foot. The movements of my legs which constitute walking do so in such a context, one that is part of the kind of life I live. In abstraction from this, I am not an intentional agent, and the movement of my legs does not constitute taking exercise or going somewhere on foot.

When Wisdom says that both thinking and walking involve the mind no less than the body, he does not mean this in the sense Descartes does. Rather, he is saying that what we consider as paradigms of the mental and the bodily in a common-or-garden sense, such as thinking and walking, cannot be conceived in separation from each other. Walking involves intention, the voluntary movement of the legs, while intention is rooted in the public life of action. As for thinking, even when it is something we do in our heads, the sense of what we do belongs to the life we share with other people. The participants of that life are, of course, *people*, with distinctively human capacities, such as the capacity for thought, reasoning and acting with intention. When we speak of a person's mind, then we are, as I said, referring to capacities like these. Human behaviour is the exercise of such capacities; it is not, as the behavioural psychologist C. L. Hull described it, 'colourless movement'.[5] The requisite bodily movements take place in the cut and thrust of human life. It is in those surroundings that they constitute human behaviour – in much the same way that, as Wittgenstein has pointed out, it is only in a human face (in the surroundings of a human face) that a smiling mouth smiles.[6]

Just one further point before I return to Davidson: I want to point out that Cartesian dualism seems to be an elaboration of the common man's way of seeing things: 'Man has a mind and a body' – both true and innocuous. All this means is that man is at one and the same time a flesh-and-blood being and a sentient creature capable of thought and judgement. Descartes, on the other hand, conceptually dissociates the mind and the body: it is the mind that thinks, feels, etc., and it is the body that moves. These movements constitute behaviour or actions in conjunction with acts of mind (acts of will); while perceptions are mental/conscious states, images, causally produced by processes in the body, these processes themselves being the result or effect of the body's causal contact with its physical environment. In other words, Descartes starts with the mind and the body in their dissociated forms – a disembodied mind, identified with the self; and the body of anatomy and physiology, a material object ('a machine fitted together and made of bones, sinews, muscles, veins, blood and skin'). He then tries to join them together, to constitute man.

This way of thinking is insidious and very difficult to get rid of. It takes philosophical work to do so, and it is in the course of such work that we shall find the illumination we need. Wittgenstein puts the point by quoting Augustine's remark that 'the search says more than the discovery'.[7] The search, in this particular case, is the journey from Cartesian dualism back to the point where our reflections began. We shall return there with an understanding that we did not (and could not) have before we fell prey to the temptations of Cartesian dualism. (Simone Weil once said that God created the world by retiring from it, so that we could cross the infinite distance he put between us and Him – the Good – and find Him. Her point was that unless a person is prepared to do the inner work – cf. the idea of self-purification in Plato's *Phaedo* – which will enable him to undertake such a spiritual journey, the only God he will find will be a worldly God, one who offers him consolations and compensations; likewise, the goodness he will find will be merely an apparent goodness, the goodness of 'the double-minded', as Kierkegaard put it.) Descartes' service to philosophy was to have the courage of his temptations and to articulate them. In articulating them so clearly and powerfully, Descartes has been a beacon in the philosophy of mind.

Let me return to Davidson's question: how can the fact that mental events resist capture in the nomological net of physical theory be reconciled with the causal role of mental events in the physical world? I connect this with a remark of his in his essay on 'Intending':

> The ontological reduction – the claim that when we act with intention, the intention with which we act is not a mysterious act of will or special attitude or episode of willing over and above the action – if it succeeds, is enough to answer many puzzles about the relation between the mind and the body, and to explain the possibility of autonomous action in a world of causality.[8]

In the essay we are currently examining – 'Mental Events', written eight years earlier – Davidson poses the same question, without the benefit of the ontological reduction: 'Reconciling freedom with causal determinism . . . entails capture in, and freedom [autonomous action] requires escape from, the nomological net [of physical theory]'.[9] Put more simply, but in the light of the same philosophical commitments, Davidson's question is: Given that, as bodily beings, we belong to (or are placed in) the physical world (a world of causality), how is it possible for us to act freely?

He says he is in sympathy with Kant, whom he quotes.[10] To paraphrase the quotation: We cannot argue freedom away. Yet we are part of nature and, as such, must be subject to natural necessity. But if we cannot argue freedom away, we must assume that there is no contradiction. Davidson's essay finishes with another quotation from Kant,[11] which I will similarly shorten and simplify: The contradiction rests on this: that we think of man in a different sense and relation when we call him free, and when we regard him as subject to the laws of nature . . . Both must be thought *as necessarily united* in the same subject. I agree with Kant and will explain below how I understand this remark.

On Davidson's account, Kant believed that freedom entails anomaly, that it fails to fall under a law.[12] As usual, Davidson's argument is cumbersome and tortuous, but I shall try to follow it to the best of my ability. He articulates three principles from which, he says, the 'apparent contradiction' stems:

1   At least some mental events interact causally with physical events. If, for instance, someone sank the *Bismarck*, he moved his body in a way that was caused by mental events of certain sorts, and this bodily movement in turn caused the sinking of the *Bismarck*. Davidson says that, where mental and physical events causally interact, perception and action provide the most obvious causes. It seems to me that Davidson is caught up in Cartesian dualism here. On the other hand, I do not believe that this is true of Kant's distinction between nature and reason.

2   'The second principle is that where there is causality, there must be a law; events related as cause and effect fall under strict deterministic laws'.[13]

3   'The third principle is that there are no strict deterministic laws on the basis of which mental events can be predicted and explained.' Davidson calls this 'the Anomalism of the Mental'.[14]

Davidson says that the paradox arises for someone who is inclined to accept these three principles but thinks of them as inconsistent. But, he goes on, all three principles seem to him to be true, and the appearance of a contradiction needs to be explained away. I say: 'Good!' Davidson also claims that this is essentially the Kantian position. I agree. But Davidson's execution of this explanatory task is an altogether different matter. This is what we must now turn to. Davidson gives a summary or preview of his argument: Section 1 'describes a version of the identity theory of the mental and the physical that shows how the three principles may be reconciled'.[15] Section 2 'argues that these cannot be strict psychophysical laws'.[16] This is entailed, he says, by the principle of anomalism of the mental. Section 3 'tries to show that from the fact that there can be no strict psychophysical laws, and our other two principles, we can infer the truth of a version of the identity theory; that is, a theory that identifies at least some mental events with physical events.'[17]

Section 1 begins with an attempt to distinguish between 'events that are mental' and 'events that are physical'. Believing, intending, desiring, helping, knowing, perceiving, noticing, remembering, Davidson says, are mental verbs. Fine. I have already said that the expression 'mental events' is an abstract philosophical expression with a Cartesian lineage. The mental, Davidson notes further along, 'exhibits intentionality'.[18] Thus, a memory is a memory of, for instance, some past event. All right – except, perhaps, for sensations like pain. What about 'physical'? Presumably, a stone falling, nerve impulses crossing synapses – these are physical events, the latter also a physiological event. So far, this is innocuous but hardly ground-breaking. Where do we go from here? We have already seen the danger ahead of us, pointed out by John Wisdom in his remark 'Aren't both, both?'!

Davidson's next step is this: 'I want to describe, and presently to argue for, a version of the identity theory that denies that there can be strict laws connecting the mental and the physical'.[19] Yet why do we need any kind of identity theory to accept such a conclusion? I suggest that Davidson needs it because, not having succeeded in dismantling Cartesian dualism, he is still operating in its gravitational field. He quotes two formulations of the identity theory, both advanced by J. J. C. Smart: 'There are not two things: a flash of lightning and an electrical discharge. There is one thing, a flash of lightning, which is described scientifically as an electrical discharge . . .'[20] So, we could say that a flash of lightning *is* an electrical discharge. Likewise, 'a sensation is a brain process'.[21] Davidson puts forward a four-fold classification of such theories in the field and opts for the fourth, which he calls 'anomalous monism'. It is, he explains, like materialism, in that it claims that 'all events are physical', aspiring to explain mental phenomena in purely physical terms. Davidson argues that anomalous monism 'allows the possibility that not all events are mental, while insisting that all events are physical'.[22] But is this not a contradiction in terms? In connection with 'the principle of the nomological character of causality', Davidson observes: 'It says that when events are related as cause and effect, they have descriptions that instantiate a law. It does not say that every true singular statement of causality instantiates a law'.[23]

I must admit that I find this kind of abstract, formalistic approach, extremely unrewarding. It reminds me of playing a game of chess in which one works out a strategy of check-mating one's opponent – in the case of philosophy, of formulating a general theory that will be impervious to various possible objections. Where does that leave one? Perhaps with a good conclusion. But what good is a conclusion in philosophy if it has not been arrived at through the kind of work that digs and opens up vistas in which one finds illumination?

I cannot resist quoting a sentence from the opening paragraph of Section 2 which I find mind-blowing:

> For if anomalous monism is correct, not only can every mental event be uniquely singled out using only physical concepts, but since the number of events that falls under each mental predicate may, for all we know, be finite, there may well exist a physical open sentence coexistence with each mental predicate, though to construct it might involve the tedium of a lengthy and uninstructive alternation.[24]

The whole section continues in this vein. One of the claims, probably the central one, that Davidson makes here is that his 'thesis is . . . that the mental is nomologically irreducible: there may be *true* general statements relating the mental and the physical, statements that have the logical form of a law, but they are not *lawlike* (in the story sense to be described)'.[25]

'A flash of lightning *is* an electric discharge.' 'A sensation is a brain process.' As I understand it, Davidson sees a similarity between the two, but also a difference. The difference, he seems to suggest, is that lightning is a physical phenomenon that could be brought under scientific discourse. When you move from talking of lightning to giving an explanation of its causation in terms of electrical discharge between two clouds, you do not change your mode of discourse, you remain within the same logical space. This could not be said when you try to explain thinking or sensation in terms of brain processes. I quote the way Davidson puts it: 'If the case of supposed laws linking the mental and the physical is different, it can only be because to allow the possibility of such laws would amount to changing the subject'.[26] Hence, he continues, 'in the case of so many other forms of definitional reductionism we should not expect nomological connections between the mental and the physical'.[27] The section ends with the conclusion that 'nomological slack between the mental and the physical is essential as long as we conceive of man as a rational animal'.[28] I feel like saying, 'I could have told you so in advance.' This is not a matter of abstract argument, but of considering human life.

Section 3 begins by reiterating that there is a categorical difference between the mental and the physical. Davidson says that this is a commonplace. I would add that there is a categorical difference between the psychological and the physiological. Davidson adds that 'the step from the categorical difference between the mental and the physical to the impossibility of strict laws relating them is less common'. He continues: 'If there is a surprise, then, it will be to find the lawlessness of the mental serving to help establish the identity of the mental with that paradigm of the lawlike, the physical'.[29] Here, I am afraid, I just do not follow.

Be that as it may, Davidson then softens 'the lawlessness of the mental' to 'there are not strict laws at all on the basis of which we can predict and explain mental phenomena'.[30] Next, he gives one of his abstract demonstrations, from which he concludes: 'So every mental event that is causally related to a physical event is a physical event.'[31] Is this true?

There are certain forms of depression that are caused by particular dysfunctions of the brain. To distinguish these from forms of depression with a purely psychological origin, the former are referred to as 'physical depressions'. This simply means that they have a physical cause. To return

to an earlier example: 'A flash of lightning *is* an electrical discharge.' I
agree. What one sees, what one calls 'a flash of lightning', is an electrical
discharge. That is what an electrical discharge looks like. In the case of a
depression whose origin is purely physical, I do not believe we can say
that this is what such-and-such a complex of events in the brain feels like.
Here, 'feels' is not a verb of perception. I would therefore say: this is the
feeling it causes. I think that the same is true of what we call 'physical
pain'. Here, the pain is a sensation caused by what happens in the body.
I am not saying that the verb 'to feel' never functions as a verb of perception – 'let me feel your pulse' – but it does not do so in the examples I
suggested.

After this grand tour of abstract surroundings, conducted by a hard
task-master, we make what I consider a soft landing: 'Two features of
mental events in their relation to the physical-causal dependence and
nomological independence – combine to dissolve what has often seemed
a paradox, the efficacy of thought and purpose in the material world, and
their freedom from law.'[32]

Let me comment on causal dependence. I agree in this sense: our thinking, for instance, is not caused by what goes on in the brain. But unless the
brain functioned properly, we could not think, at any rate not properly. By
contrast, what happens in the brain can cause hallucinations.

I think that by the nomological independence of the mental, Davidson
means that we cannot explain 'mental, psychological phenomena' by what
happens in the brain; or that we cannot reduce psychology to physiology.
So, if I have understood Davidson properly on these two points, I agree.
But I certainly do not follow how he has steered us to this conclusion.

As for the paradox surrounding 'the efficacy of thought and purpose
in the material world, and their freedom from law',[33] Davidson explains:
'When we portray events as perceivings, rememberings, decisions and
actions, we necessarily locate them amid physical happenings through
the relation of cause and effect'.[34] Before continuing with what Davidson
writes, let me briefly try to say what I understand. We are flesh-and-blood
beings, with an anatomy and a physiology. The latter's proper functioning
is essential to our capacity to act, to think, to judge, to feel, to be in per-
ceptual and sensory contact with our environment. That environment is
to a large extent physical, although it is suffused with social significances.

So, even though we live in a social world, the world of our culture, we
are constantly in contact with the world of physical objects and physical
processes. Therefore, we are subject to causal interactions from both ends:
through the functioning of our physiology and through our physical
contacts with the objects that surround us. I said 'we are subject to causal

interactions', but that doesn't mean that we are governed by them. I think that is what Davidson says, in his own way, in the remainder of the above quotation. What he expresses there is what he calls 'the nomological independence of the mental', of the psychological. 'Mental events as a class', he continues, 'cannot be explained by physical science; particular mental events can when we know [their] particular identities.'[35]

We have already seen this; we cannot explain acting, thinking, judging, reasoning, etc., causally, the way physical events are explained in the physical sciences. But we can explain certain hallucinations, certain kinds of depression, etc. this way. The former presuppose the proper functioning of our physiology. For instance, we cannot lift our arm to greet someone if we are paralysed. The hallucinations, for example, that are explained causally, are the effects of the *failure* of our physiology to function properly. This is part of our being flesh-and-blood beings.

Davidson continues: 'But the explanations of mental events in which we are typically interested relate them to other mental events and conditions.'[36] In other words, they have a psychological explanation. 'Such accounts [explanations]', he continues, 'operate in a conceptual framework removed from the direct reach of physical law . . .'[37] I agree wholeheartedly. In lieu of the dots, Davidson has the words, 'by describing both cause and effect, and reason and action, as aspects of a portrait of a human agent'. When he says 'cause and effect', I am not sure what he has in mind. Davidson then goes on: 'The anomalism of the mental is thus a necessary condition for viewing action as autonomous.'[38]

By 'autonomous', I understand 'coming from the agent', 'not dictated or caused by anything external to him or his will, the will he owns and which, therefore, is his'. The reason I put it like this is that there are cases where a person is under someone else's domination, for instance, but deceives himself into thinking that he does what he wants when, in reality, he reluctantly serves the other. This is one of the many different kinds of examples of psychological determinism. Thus, when a person is subject to what I call a 'determining psychology' and is not free in what he does, his actions are determined by something external to him, although this involves his complicity in bad faith. That is why he can shake off his fetters and come to himself. This takes inner work, a motive for him to undertake it, and of course honesty.

Davidson concludes with a quotation from Kant. We have already seen that there are at least two different senses in which a man is subject to the laws of nature, and I think that Kant is aware of both. One, which Davidson also has in mind, is our dependence on the proper functioning of our bodies, our physiology. The other one is the lure of the self (in the sense of 'self' as it appears in expressions like 'selfish', 'self-centred', etc.). This is sometimes referred to as 'the flesh' or 'nature', as opposed to 'the soul' or 'the spiritual'. I have argued elsewhere that Kant's contrast between 'phenomenal reality' and 'noumenal reality' in his ethics – *not* in his epistemology – is the same contrast.[39] We have the same contrast in Simone Weil's distinction between 'the natural' and 'the supernatural' or 'spiritual'. The natural, she says, is subject to moral gravity – a form of psychological determinism – and pulls us morally down (in a 'secondary sense' of 'down') towards 'baseness'; whereas, when we are able to turn away from what is selfish, self-interested, or self-centred in us, we are freed by 'grace', rise morally, and find our soul. As I have argued above, in finding our soul we come to ourselves and find autonomy. Our psychology is transformed into an 'enabling psychology'. This is the topic of my book, *Good and Evil, and their Respective Psychologies*.[40] I mention this in connection with the Kantian question with which Davidson ends his essay.

As I said, I wholeheartedly agree with the conclusions of Davidson's essay 'Mental Events', but am amazed at the route he takes to reach them. That it is so circuitous is, I think, partly the result of the vestiges of Cartesian dualism with which he is struggling.

2. Psychology as Philosophy

The title of this essay is puzzling. Davidson presents an excuse for using it which I do not accept; but I shall return to this at the end of my discussion.

In this paper, Davidson is concerned with the character of psychology as a discipline and, in particular, with the question whether it is a science: 'Can intentional human behaviour be explained and predicted in the same way other phenomena are?'[41] He says that there is a pull in two opposite directions and articulates the following antinomy: (a) 'On the one hand human acts are clearly part of the order of nature, causing and being caused by events outside ourselves.'[42] (b) 'On the other hand, there are good arguments against the view that thought, desire and voluntary action can be brought under deterministic laws, as physical phenomena can.'[43] Davidson comments: 'An adequate theory of behaviour must do justice to both these insights and show how, contrary to appearance, they can be reconciled.'[44]

Let me say straightaway that (a) holds no attraction for me. Are human acts part of the order of nature in the sense in which Davidson means this? I thought he had abandoned this idea. The fact that human action presupposes the proper functioning of the physiological body does not make human acts 'part of the order of nature'. We sink into nature, in this sense, when we become ill, when our body stops functioning properly.

Sartre speaks of the body as 'invisible' to us when we act; and when, by contrast, we are debilitated by an illness and our body becomes a burden to us, he says that 'the corpse appears in our body' or 'in us'.

With regard to (b), Davidson says that 'by evaluating the arguments against the possibility of deterministic laws of behaviour, we can test the claims of psychology to be a science like others (some others)'.[45] Good, except that what one needs here is not the evaluation of arguments, but common sense and reflection. Let me first make a distinction which Davidson, it seems to me, skates over. There are two different ways in which psychology may be thought to be a science. According to the first, it would be a science – experimental psychology – if there were 'deterministic laws of behaviour'. If there were such laws, it would be a science, in much the same sense in which the early Freud thought of it in 'A Project for a Scientific Psychology'. In the latter case, psychology would be a branch of physiology.

In the next paragraph, Davidson jumps to the second way in which psychology may be thought to be a science. He writes:

What lies behind our inability to discover deterministic psycho-physical laws is this. When we attribute a belief, a desire, a goal, an intention or a meaning to an agent, we necessarily operate within a system of concepts in part determined by the structure of beliefs and desires of the agent himself. Short of changing the subject, we cannot escape this feature of the psychological; but this feature has no counterpart in the world of physics.[46]

I would say: Right on the dot! But why did it take so long for Davidson to get here? I have already suggested why. Next, he says, again quite correctly, that

the nomological irreducibility of the psychological means . . . that the social sciences cannot be expected to develop in ways exactly parallel to the physical sciences, nor can we expect ever to be able to explain and predict human behaviour with the kind of precision that is possible in principle for physical phenomena.[47]

I would put this more boldly: Psychology is not a science; a lot of time has been wasted in treating it as such, and much that is silly and stupid has been said and written as a result. Even in my limited experience it seems to me that a great deal of academic psychology has been corrupted by such scientism.[48] Davidson goes on:

This does not mean that there are any events that are in themselves undetermined or unpredictable, it is only events as described in the vocabulary of thought and action that resist incorporation into a closed deterministic system. These same events, described in appropriate physical terms, are as amenable to prediction and explanation as any.[49]

It is not clear to me what Davidson is saying here. Suppose a man lifts up his arm to say 'Hello' to greet me. This is an action. Davidson says that this action [not event] resists incorporation into a closed deterministic system. All right. What '*same event*', then, 'described in appropriate physical terms' is 'amenable to prediction and explanation'? The physical, bodily movement? Yes, that movement is made possible by the neuro-physiological processes in the anatomical body. If it were a reflex movement, then it would, indeed, be amenable to prediction and causal, deterministic explanation.

But in this case the action, the greeting, is *not* a reflex movement. The most that could be said is that it is the same part of the body that enters into the action as the one which, on a completely different occasion, enters into the reflex movement. It is the same part of the body that moves, but the movement is not the same. In the one case, the man moves his arm; in the other, the same arm moves of its own accord, because it has been tapped on the elbow. The arm is the same, but the occasions in which it moves are *not* the same, nor do we have the same movement. At best, Davidson has expressed himself very badly here.

He goes on to talk about the three premises of a particular argument for monism. According to the first, 'psychological events such as perceivings, rememberings, the acquisition and loss of knowledge, and intentional actions are directly or indirectly caused by, and the causes of physical events'.[50] There are causal processes involved, of course, but these are not the direct or even indirect cause of what we perceive. What makes seeing possible involves a lot of learning. Seeing is not the having of visual sensations. We can only see what we have learned to recognize, to identify. I should like to quote two separate paragraphs from an early book of mine, where I discuss perception:

Seeing . . . requires a subject – a person or an animal. It is *I* who see the table, or it is the dog who does so. That is, a subject who can act, recognize and identify things and react to them in certain ways. We can attribute seeing only to a creature who behaves in some ways comparable to human beings, a creature who responds to the objects of sight in distinctive ways. This is what is of primary importance for attributing perception to a creature, and not any process that goes on in his body.[51]

. . .

The physiological processes which our organs of perception, the eyes, support are necessary to vision in the sense that a man with a detached retina cannot see. He cannot see in the same sense that a man paralysed with a spinal injury cannot move his legs. We can say, 'His nerves must be intact if he is able to move his limbs at will' and similarly, 'His optic nerve, retina and so on must be in working order if he is to be able to see'. But voluntary movements are learned, and so is seeing, at least it presupposes such that we acquire by learning. We acquire the capacity to see, and we do so together with the capacity to move in various ways voluntarily, to respond to objects, to act, to touch, handle and manipulate them.[52]

For the reasons I have given above, I cannot agree with the first premise of Davidson's argument. The second premise says that 'when events are related as cause and effect, then there exists a closed and deterministic system of laws into which these events, when appropriately described, fit'.[53] The third premise is that 'there are no precise psycho-physical laws.'[54] All right. I will not bother to quote the rest of the paragraph, nor can I go through every sentence with a toothpick. I honestly think that the abstract wranglings in which Davidson engages in order to reach his conclusions are futile. 'Anomalous' or not, I cannot agree with his monism.

'My general strategy', Davidson writes, 'for trying to show that there are no strict psychophysical laws depends, first, on emphasizing the holistic character of the cognitive field'.[55] This, if I understand it correctly, at least chimes in with what I said earlier in connection with perception. 'These conditions', Davidson now, 'have no echo in physical theory, which is why we can look for no more than a rough correlation between psychological and physical phenomena.' I agree, except that I would not describe the relation between the psychological and the physical in terms of a 'correlation'. I would say that the physical or physiological here is a necessary condition for the psychological to take effect: if I am to see, my retina must be in place; if I am to be able to lift my arm so as to greet someone, my arm must not be paralysed.

I am not sure, however, that this is what Davidson has in mind. For in the examples he gives of Achilles wanting to avenge the death of

Patroclus, and of Oedipus killing his father, Davidson reverts to talking of beliefs and desires as causes of our actions. A little further on, he talks of a reason as a 'rational cause'.[56] He then says that 'there are no serious laws connecting reasons and actions'. I completely accept what he takes this to lead to, namely that

> it is an error to compare a truism like 'if a man wants to eat an acorn omelette, then he generally will if the opportunity exists and no other desire overrides' with a law that says how fast a body will fall in a vacuum.[57]

But did we have to go through all this heavy weather to see this? In any case, and as I said earlier, it is a mistake to identify reasons with causes. In my view, Davidson's essay 'Psychology as Philosophy' contains a lot of hot air. The reason is, I think, the same as that which applies to the previous essay, namely Davidson's Cartesian lineage, probably also his scientistic lineage. He wishes to turn away from both, but without dismantling them. Instead, he takes the high road of abstract argument, which takes him along a tortuous path.

Earlier in this chapter, I spoke of Davidson's conclusion as a 'soft landing'. Here, too, what he says in conclusion is eminently sensible, namely that (i) there are no 'serious laws connecting reasons and actions', no strict predictions of human actions, and that (ii) we cannot turn this mode of explanation [i.e. psychological explanation of human actions and behaviour] into something more like science'.[58] Davidson also speaks of 'the irreducibility of psychological concepts'.[59] I do not know what or how much he retracts when he notes in his 'Comments and Replies' that he did not intend to make an attack on psychology generally, or at least on its right to be called a science.[60] Nor do I see why Davidson is afraid to deny psychology this right. The way he puts it is that 'psychology is set off from other sciences in an important and interesting way'.[61] Well, I have already said what I think.

Davidson also writes – and I am not sure that I have got this right – that when he realized that human choices cannot be predicted accurately, and recognized that it was 'impossible to construct a formal theory that could explain this', he gave up his career as an experimental psychologist.[62] He notes that the 'conclusion is rather that psychology is set off from other sciences in an important and interesting way. The argument against the existence of strict psychophysical laws provides the key to psychology's uniqueness'.[63] All right, but experimental psychology recognizes this and still insists that it is an experimental science. I thought that Davidson was disenchanted with experimental psychology – as he should be, on the basis of some of the things he says.

Now, about the oddity of the title of the essay I have been discussing: 'Psychology as Philosophy', Davidson writes:

> In the formulation of hypotheses and the reading of evidence, there is no way psychology can avoid consideration of the nature of rationality, of coherence and consistency. At one end of the spectrum, logic and rational decision theory are psychological theories from which the obviously empirical has been drained. At the other end, there is some form of behaviourism better imagined than described from which all taint of the normative has been subtracted. Psychology, if it deals with propositional attitudes, hovers in between. This branch of the subject cannot be divorced from such questions as what constitutes a good argument, a valid inference, a rational plan, or a good reason for acting. These questions also belong to the traditional concerns of philosophy, which is my excuse for my title.[64]

I would not put what Davidson is trying to say in this way. Psychology as a discipline, and the training and education of psychologists, have a great deal to learn from philosophy. There was a time, when I was a graduate student, that a course in psychology was part of the Moral Science tripos in Cambridge. When, a few years later, I started teaching philosophy, the study of psychology was carried on in the philosophy department. This was mutually beneficial. Some years later, I taught part of a course in philosophical psychology to psychology undergraduates. Influenced by their teachers, most of the students resented this because it reduced the time they had for the study of psychology. A minority greatly appreciated it. In our technological culture, this trend of regarding psychology as a science to which the study of philosophy could be nothing but an intrusion has hardened, to the great impoverishment of the discipline of psychology.

Obviously, psychology and philosophy are different disciplines, but philosophy has much to contribute to psychology. It can make the difference between a thoughtless and a *thoughtful* psychology. What I call a 'thoughtful psychology' is one that gives time to reflecting on both life as it is actually lived by human beings, and on the distinctive character of human life. What has developed into 'experimental psychology' sees no difference between human beings and animals, nor between different animals. More recently, the difference between human beings and machines – computers and robots – has also come to be eroded. This latter development belongs to our technological culture. I agree with what Davidson says about our limited ability to predict human actions and want to finish my discussion of 'Psychology as Philosophy' by quoting two paragraphs from my book on *Free Will*.[65] They constitute the conclusion of Chapter 15:

> In reality, of course, what we can predict about others is very limited – for instance, we can predict that someone will vote for a certain party at the coming election; but normally not the sequence of the things he will say during a conversation. This has to do with the difference between a conversation and a drill for instance. I said 'normally'. If what he said in this way was predictable then we could not carry out a conversation with him. There are, of course, people who to some extent approximate this. We would say of them, if only metaphorically, that they were 'brain damaged'. Conversation would not exist in a community of such 'brain damaged' people . . .
>
> As for predicting what one will oneself do, that too is the exception rather than the rule – for instance that when one is offered a drink one will not be able to say no. Here we have a variety of cases of compulsion and addiction. These are cases which constitute 'the abnormal'. Normally, when I say what I will do next, I am not predicting my behaviour; what I do is to declare my intention. Here it is *I* who make what I say come true by *doing* what I say I will do. What I do is not something that happens to me, something I observe or predict. As I said, my will may on certain kinds of situations be determined, and I may even not recognize this to be the case. But this does not make me an automaton, for it is as an intentional agent that I am being manipulated, it is in my will that I am a captive to something external to it. Furthermore this in general must be the exception rather than the rule. Otherwise I could not even *think* that I was an automaton; and neither could anyone *say* it of me.[66]

3.   The Material Mind

'The Material Mind' is an exercise from which Davidson again draws the conclusion that 'there is no important sense in which psychology can be reduced to the physical sciences.'[67] On this point we are in agreement. Davidson begins by saying, 'suppose that we understand what goes on in the brain perfectly', and 'while we are dreaming, let us also dream that the brain, and associated nervous system, have come to be understood as operating much like a computer'. Further, 'let us imagine *l'homme machine* has actually been built, out of the very stuff of a man.'[68] Our evidence is that 'everything we can learn about the physical structure and workings of actual human brains and bodies has been replicated, and that Art (as I shall call him or it) has acted in all observable ways like a man'.[69] I would like to add: for this scenario to work we would have to imagine a long stretch of time with Art in situations that belong to human life, e.g. Art talking, communicating, responding, carrying out a conversation with others. Indeed, we have to imagine interacting with and sharing a life with Art. We have seen films of this kind.

I do not believe that this exercise in imagination will take us anywhere new. Indeed, Davidson comes to the same conclusion: 'We see, then, that complete knowledge of the physics of man . . . does not . . . yield knowledge of psychology'.[70] 'Still', Davidson asks, 'why should it not happen that there are inductively established correlations between physical and psychological events?'[71] As I pointed out earlier, what we have are not 'correlations'. What is needed for a person to act, think, see, etc., is that his body should be in good working order. The correlations, if that is the word to use, are between various parts of the brain and various types of movements, forms of thinking, etc. Davidson continues: 'Nevertheless, our detailed understanding of the physical workings cannot, in itself, force us to conclude that Art is angry, or that he believes Beethoven died in Vienna'.[72] Of course not. Davidson makes various statements of this sort. However, what is needed is a discussion of the question 'Why not?' True, Davidson points out that to assume that 'Art is processing . . . is to fit what we thus assume into the total picture'.[73] But this needs elaboration. Further on, Davidson writes:

> If we want to know whether a particular one of these [bodily movements] will be interpretable as an action or a response, we can tell only by considering all the physical aspects in detail (including of course what the environment will be like) and then judging the case as we would a human movement.[74]

I do not see that the physical environment in itself is of great relevance. What is important is the context, the situation, and the sense it has in the kind of life in which the agent participates, his behaviour and his responses over a period of time, and the ways in which these are connected. How can a computerized puppet be made to pass such a test? It does not live the life of a human being; it merely copies the life of one who does. It has been programmed to do so. Davidson considers various arguments – to no avail. 'We must interpret the whole pattern', he says.[75] I would add: 'Not to mention the temporal dimension of the pattern'. Davidson then asks:

'Can we not locate *the physical correlates of meaning*? Can we not discover unambiguously on the physical level what we must merely infer, or treat as a construct, as long as we stick to observation of speech behaviour?'[76] He comes out with a negative answer: 'A few questions like this should make us realize that we cannot simply associate some fixed part of Art's brain, or aspect of it, with the criteria for the application of a word'.[77] Davidson's conclusion, not surprisingly, is negative:

> Detailed knowledge of the physics or physiology of the brain, indeed of the whole man, would not provide a shortcut to the kind of inter- pretation required for the application of sophisticated psychological concepts . . . There is no important sense in which psychology can be reduced to the physical sciences.[78]

I agree; but again I do not find this exercise very rewarding. Why not? I suppose it is because the arguments look at the human situation from on high. Davidson has a facility for general descriptions and abstract argu- ments. He is a 'high flyer' – a term generally used so as to praise. But in philosophy I prefer someone who digs patiently. Here I would contrast Davidson with Melden. Melden has no pretensions, but he is sound, and when I read his *Free Action*, I find greater illumination. If I may put it this way: Instead of dismantling fashionable positions, Davidson shoots them down. But it is the dismantling that liberates us and simultaneously brings us understanding, insight. Argument forces our hand; the dismantling of attractive-sounding positions changes our perspective and makes us see what we did not appreciate before.

Finally, a point that I'll just state without developing it: I believe that there is a way of philosophizing that involves more than the intellect. Conceptual though philosophical discussion may be, it can open up in us an understanding of human life, its character and problems. This has been my own, personal experience of philosophy. I think and hope that this is apparent in my writings.

Notes

1 Donald Davidson, *Essays on Actions and Events* (Oxford: Clarendon Press, 1980), 207.
2 Ibid.
3 Ibid.
4 John Wisdom, *Other Minds* (Oxford: Blackwell, 1952), 223.
5 C. L. Hull, *Principles of Behavior* (New York: Appleton-Century-Crofts, 1943), 25.

6 Ludwig Wittgenstein, *Philosophical Investigations*, trans. G. E. M. Anscombe (Oxford: Blackwell, 1999), §583.

7 Idem, *Zettel*, ed. G. H. von Wright and G. E. M. Anscombe, trans. G. E. M. Anscombe (Oxford: Blackwell, 1981), §457.

8 Davidson, *Essays on Actions and Events*, 88.

9 Ibid., 207.

10 Ibid., The quote is from Immanuel Kant, *Fundamental Principles of the Metaphysics of Morals*, trans. T. K. Abbot (London: Longman, Green and Co., 1909), 75–6.

11 Davidson, *Essays on Actions and Events*, 225.

12 Ibid.

13 Ibid., 208.

14 Ibid.

15 Ibid., 209

16 Ibid.

17 Ibid.

18 Ibid., 211.

19 Ibid., 212.

20 Ibid., cf. J. J. C. Smart, 'Sensations and Brain Processes', in *Philosophical Review*, 68 (1959): 141–56. Reprinted in V. C. Chappell (ed.), *Philosophy of Mind* (Englewood Cliffs, N.J., 1962), 163–5.

21 Ibid.

22 Davidson, *Essays on Actions and Events*, 214.

23 Ibid., 215.

24 Ibid., 215–16.

25 Ibid., 216.

26 Ibid.

27 Ibid., 217.

28 Ibid., 223.

29 Ibid.

30 Ibid., 224.

31 Ibid.

32 Ibid., 224–5.

33 Ibid., 225.

34 Ibid.

35 Ibid.

36 Ibid.

37 Ibid.

38 Ibid.

39 See Ilham Dilman, *Wittgenstein's Copernican Revolution* (London: Palgrave, 2000), Chs. 3, 4, and 5.

40 Ilham Dilman, *The Self, the Soul and the Psychology of Good and Evil* (London: Routledge, 2005).

41 Davidson, *Essays on Actions and Events*, 230.

42 Ibid.

43 Ibid.

44 Ibid.

45 Ibid.

46 Ibid.

47 Ibid.

48 See the first three chapters in my book *Raskolnikov's Rebirth: Psychology and the Understanding of Good and Evil* (Chicago, Ill.: Open Court, 2000), entitled 'Science and Psychology', 'The Psychology of Moral Behaviour', and 'Psychology and Morality'.

49 Davidson, *Essays on Actions and Events*, 230.

50 Ibid., 231.

51 Ilham Dilman, *Love and Human Separateness* (Oxford: Blackwell, 1987), 21.

52 Ibid., 25.

53 Davidson, *Essays on Actions and Events*, 231.

54 Ibid.

55 Ibid.

56 Ibid., 232.

57 Ibid., 233.

58 Ibid.

59 Ibid., 241.

60 Ibid., 240.

61 Ibid., 241.

62 Ibid., 236.

63 Ibid., 241.

64 Ibid.

65 See Ilham Dilman, *Free Will* (London: Routledge, 1999)

66 Davidson, *Essays on Actions and Events*, 253–4.

67 Ibid., 259.

68 Ibid., 245.

69 Ibid.

70 Ibid., 250.

71 Ibid.

72 Ibid.

73 Ibid. I would rather put the claim that 'Art is processing information' in terms of his learning to do things, to recognize, to appreciate, etc.

74 Ibid., 251.

75 Ibid., 257.
76 Ibid., 258.
77 Ibid.
78 Ibid., 258–9.

6   Robert Nozick's Philosophical Meditations

I

As I explained in my introduction, my choice of authors and particular works to be discussed was the result of chance. In each case, I wanted the author to be someone who has come to be well known, and with whom I thought I would disagree. The latter does not apply to Nozick, however. I had not read any of his works. An American friend of mine recommended *The Examined Life: Philosophical Meditations* to me, and I thought – rightly, as it turned out – that it would be different from what one would expect from a professional philosopher, at least in the narrow sense of that term.

In his Introduction, Nozick rightly observes that 'life or living is not the kind of topic whose investigation philosophers find especially rewarding'.[1] Towards the end of the Introduction, after mentioning Descartes, Kant, Nietzsche, Kierkegaard, Pascal and Plotinus, Nozick writes: 'The predominant current perspective on philosophy has been "cleansed" to leave a tradition in which the rational mind speaks (only) to the rational mind'.[2] I know what he means, and I agree. Nozick adds that 'there is no overwhelming reason to limit all of philosophy to that'.[3] Again, I agree.

Nozick describes the chapters of his book as 'philosophical meditations'. They are meditations or reflections – not quite the same thing, perhaps – and are philosophical in that they centre on certain kinds of questions. They prompt Nozick to draw certain distinctions, particularly between what is genuine and what is not, between mere appearance (deceptive appearance) and reality, and also between what is shallow and what is deep. In addition to drawing these distinctions, Nozick also tries to throw light on them. He covers a range of topics, some of which are connected and contribute to a sort of progression. It is also true that the topics of Nozick's meditations focus on aspects of life that raise certain difficulties, viz. philosophical difficulties. Some of his remarks express his own, personal response to life. They are the responses of a person who has thought about life and grown in that thinking. I like especially what he says at the end of his penultimate chapter, entitled 'Philosophy's Life'. I quote only a few sentences:

Love of this world is co-ordinated with love of life. Life is our being in this world. And love of life is our fullest response to being alive, our fullest way of exploring what it is to be alive . . . This love of life is continuous with an appreciation of life's energy in its various forms, with the variety and tolerance and interplay of life in nature. Appreciating this, we will not wantonly exploit animal or plant life; we will take some care to minimize the damage we do . . . as part of nature and its cycles, we can repay our debt for what we take . . . What constitutes us is had on loan.[4]

I also like what Nozick says (in the opening pages of Chapter 22) about humanity's great spiritual leaders. Again, I quote just three sentences:

The spiritual teachers are exemplars of the full force of their values. Part of their appeal is the appeal of these high values, but another part is the extraordinary reality the spiritual teachers achieve as archetypes and embodiments of these values. It is as if the values as Platonic Forms have been made incarnate here on earth.[5]

In a short chapter entitled 'A Portrait of the Philosopher as a Young Man', Nozick relates how, when he was 15 or 16 years old, he would carry around in the streets of Brooklyn a paperback copy of Plato's *Republic*, front cover facing outward: 'I sometimes wonder, not without uneasiness, what that young man of fifteen or sixteen would think of what he has grown up to do. I would like to think that with this book he would be pleased'.[6] I do not know Nozick's wider œuvre and contribution to philosophy, so I cannot respond to the first of the two sentences I have quoted. I also find it difficult to respond to the second. Certainly, *The Examined Life* contains much that the young man in Brooklyn should be pleased with, most notably what it conveys about the kind of person this young man, who carried Plato's *Republic* in his pocket, has developed into. This doesn't mean, however, that I do not have philosophical reservations about what Nozick has written here. I genuinely wish it were otherwise.

II

The contents of the first nine chapters are varied. This is not meant to be a criticism. From Chapter 2 ('Dying'), I select just one of Nozick's remarks: 'How unwilling someone is to die should depend, I think, upon what he has left undone, and also upon his remaining capacity to do things'.[7] Considering where I am now, I share this sentiment. 'Some', Nozick continues, 'undergo much torment before dying; weak, unable to walk or turn in bed unaided, constantly in pain, frightened, demoralized.'[8] Yes, I would not wish this on anyone, and though I am not afraid of death, the prospect of such torment does frighten me. Nozick goes on:

> After we have done all we can to help, we can share with them the *fact of* their suffering. They need not suffer alone; whether or not this makes the suffering less painful, it makes it more bearable. We also can share the fact of someone's dying, reducing temporarily the way death cuts off connection to others. Sharing someone's dying, we realize that someday we may share with others the fact of *our* dying.[9]

Yes, this is very true. I also agree with what Nozick subsequently describes as the starker truth, namely that 'this life is the only existence there is'.[10] There is still the question of what sense to make of the religious belief regarding an afterlife. I am not saying that the belief is senseless; I ask – though not here – what sense does it make?

Chapter 4 of Nozick's book ('Creating'), emphasizes that creativity is 'self-transforming'. It is 'self-transforming', so I would add, because it is a form of *giving*. It is, as Nozick points out, intensive work. He notes, as did Wittgenstein, that it is 'work upon the self' or 'a working on oneself'. It is a working on oneself because one leaves the beaten track, because one closely identifies oneself with what one is searching for, so that the latter's destiny becomes one's own. Moreover, the work and its progress calls for special moral qualities – patience, courage, trust in the midst of solitude. Creativity has its rewards, but it has trials and hazards which one can only face alone. To be honest, I found Chapter 5 ('The Nature of God, the Nature of Faith') rather orthodox and unenlightening, nor do I have anything special to say about Chapter 10 ('The Holiness of Everyday Life'). Halfway through the chapter, Nozick writes:

> We open ourselves, also, to the specific character of the food, to the taste and texture, and so to the inner quality of the substance. I want to speak of the purity and dignity of an apple, the explosive joy and sexuality of a strawberry.[11]

Nozick adds that we have a mode of knowing these things in their inner essence. Here, I can't resist quoting from Rilke's *Sonnets to Orpheus*:

> Banana, rounded apple, russet pear,
> gooseberry . . . Does not all this convey
> life and death into your mouth? . . . It's there! . . .

> Read it on a child's face any day, when it tastes them.[12]
> Stay, . . . this is good . . . But already it's flown.
> . . . Murmurs of music, a footing, a humming: -
> Maidens, so warm, so mute, are you coming
> to dance the taste of this fruit we've known?
> Dance the orange. Who can forget it,
> the way it would drown in itself, – how, too,
> it would struggle against its sweetness. And yet
> it's been yours. Been deliciously changed into you.[13]

Of course, one has to be a poet to convey what Nozick means by the 'inner essence' of the strawberry and its taste. But a philosopher, too, can help to clarify matters. Unfortunately, a philosopher's contribution often takes the form of muddying the waters without adding much – if anything – to our understanding. Next in Nozick's book comes a chapter on sexuality, which contains a number of good points. I will simply mention them here. 'What is exciting [in sex] is interpersonal', Nozick says.[14] The point is well developed in the remainder of the chapter:

> It is exciting to know another is attuned to your sensations as keenly as you are. A partner's delicacy of motion and response can show knowledge of your pleasure and care about its details.[15] . . . It is not surprising that profound emotions are awakened and expressed in sex. The trust involved in showing our own pleasures, the vulnerability in letting another give us these and guide them, including pleasures with infantile or oedipal reverberations, or anal ones, does not come lightly.[16]
> The partners see their strongest and most primitive emotions expressed and also contained safely. It is not only the other person who is known more deeply in sex. One knows one's own self better in experiencing what it is capable of: passion, love, aggression, vulnerability, domination, playfulness, infantile pleasure, joy. The depth of relaxing afterward is a measure of the fullness and profundity of the experience together, and a part of it.[17]
> The realm of sex is or can be inexhaustible. There is no limit to what can be learned and felt about each other in sex; the only limit is the sensitivity or responsiveness or creativity or daring of the partners. There always are new depths – and new surfaces – to be explored . . . Sex also is a mode of communication, a way of saying or of showing something more telling than our words can say.[18]

Nozick continues: 'Like musicians in jazz improvisation, sexual partners are engaged in a dialogue, partly scored, partly improvised, where each very attentively responds to the statements in the bodily motions of the other'.[19] He also writes:

> Through the layers of public defences and faces, another is admitted to see a more vulnerable or a more impassioned you. Nothing is more intimate than showing another your physical pleasure, perhaps because we learned we had to hide it even (or especially) from our parents. Once inside the maintained boundaries, new intimacies are possible.[20]

There are similar remarks about 'simultaneous orgasms'. I would call this a decent chapter, even though it covers just six pages. It is followed by a longer one, entitled 'Love's Bond'. To me, this is a more interesting chapter, not least because it raises some philosophical questions. By 'love's bond' is meant the bond which love creates between two people who love each other.

Nozick begins by noting that there are different kinds of love, for instance parental love, a child's love for his parents, love of one's country, and sexual love, to which Nozick refers to as 'romantic love'. I would also add the love of friends for each other, as well as compassion. But Nozick concentrates on romantic or sexual love. What is common to all love, he says, is the way the lover's well-being comes to be tied up with that of the beloved. 'When something bad happens to one you love . . . something bad also happens *to you*.'[21] Nozick describes this in terms of sharing a new identity: 'The people you love are included inside your boundaries, their well-being is your own'.[22] Indeed, 'it feels to the two people that they have united to form and constitute a new identity in the world, what might be called a *we*'.[23]

Nozick continues: 'People who form a *we* pool not only their well-being but also their autonomy'.[24] With regard to the former, he says: 'Thus, love places a floor under your well-being; it provides insurance in the face of fate's blows'.[25] He explains:

> Bad things that happen to your loved one happen to you. But so too do good things; moreover, someone who loves you helps you with care and comfort to meet vicissitudes – not out of selfishness although her doing so does, in part, help maintain her own well-being too.[26]

This is what Nozick means by 'love placing a floor under your well-being'. I need to point out that this poses a risk to one's love, insofar as it may taint it with a corrupting influence.

No doubt there is a distinction between the kind of sacrificial love that characterizes religious and spiritual love, and romantic or sexual love. But I would say that romantic love is a stage in sexual love. As sexual love becomes deeper – and it does not have to lose its sexual character for this to happen – it acquires a spiritual aspect, without any divide. Love does not have to be fully giving; there are different degrees of giving. But the more giving it is, the more is the lover willing and capable to make sacrifices for the beloved. Still, where love is mutual and part of a relationship, it develops within that relationship. To take an extreme case: where the beloved is exploitative, this places a limit on its development and on the form in which it can be maintained by the lover whose love is a giving one.

Returning to Nozick's distinction between forming a *we* in which lovers pool their identity, and a *we* in which they pool their autonomy, I think that both involve dangers. A line from a poem by Ezra Pound comes to mind: 'I want to bathe in your foreignness', i.e. in your otherness. Good, but it is important that the beloved – if it is the beloved who speaks this line – should keep her distinct identity. Of course, lover and beloved grow together in the give-and-take of their relationship. But they can grow together in the way they care for each other without losing their individual identity. This is a very delicate balance.

As for pooling their autonomy together, I think this involves greater dangers. Let us not confuse this with the lovers deciding on a division of labour, with each assuming responsibility for different aspects of their life together. Handing one's autonomy over to the other is a form of passivity and, indeed, of ungiving. On the other hand, taking over someone's autonomy is ruling the other, showing no respect for the other as an independent individual.

Love's bond must not be allowed to be determined by the lovers' psychologies. Lover and beloved must work on it individually, in the solitude of their soul, but also in harmony, by remaining honest and open with each other. An element of luck and, of course, good judgement and decency, also play a part. I suppose this is what Nozick means when he says: 'To love someone might be, in part, to devote alertness to their well-being and your connection with them'.[27] I shall now quote part of a paragraph in which Nozick seems to me to be insufficiently critical:

> This [the desire to possess the other *completely*] does not have to stem from a desire to dominate the other as completely as you do your own identity. This is an expression of the fact that you *are* forming a new identity with him or her. Or, perhaps, this desire just *is* the desire to form an identity with the other. Unlike Hegel's description

of the unstable dialectic between the master and the slave, though, in a romantic *we* the autonomy of the other and complete possession too are reconciled in the formation of a joint and wondrous enlarged identity for both.[28]

By way of a counterpoint, I would like to quote from the Preface to my book *Love: Its Forms, Dimensions and Paradoxes*:[29]

Is the desire for oneness which is at the heart of sexual love an expression of immaturity? And can the lovers who are drawn to one another find the oneness they long for? Sartre thinks that this oneness which we long for in love is a pipedream . . . His answer is that the lover must learn to live in conflict with the other and maintain his freedom or autonomy as an individual. Erich Fromm and Gabriel Marcel which the present book discusses in separate chapters make a distinction between 'symbiotic union' or 'fusion without integrity' and 'union with integrity' (Fromm) or 'communion' (Marcel).

Simone Weil appreciates the difficulty which Sartre articulates. She writes: 'When a human being is attached to another by a bond of affection which contains any degree of necessity, it is impossible that he should wish autonomy to be preserved both in himself and in the other'.[30] She attributes this to 'the mechanism of nature'.[31] However, she (Simone Weil) believes that in such a situation what is impossible can be made possible by 'the miraculous intervention of the supernatural'. This brings a change in the lovers' affective focus with a loss of its self-centred orientation. As a result they are able (as she puts it) to 'fully consent to be two and not one'. They learn to 'respect the distance which the fact of being two distinct creatures places between them'.[32] As Kahlil Gibran puts it:
But let there be spaces in your togetherness,
And let the winds of the heavens dance between you.[33]

I'll briefly comment on Simone Weil's discussion of friendship. She says that, when friendship is pure, i.e. unsoiled by the wish to please or to dominate, it is 'a miracle by which a person consents to view from a certain distance, and without coming any nearer, the very being who is necessary to him as food'.[34] Let me explain what she means by 'the miraculous intervention of the supernatural'. By the natural in us – or 'human nature' – Weil means needs that are deeply entrenched in our being – such as the need to assert ourselves, to compensate for a humiliation which deflates the ego, to respond in kind, so as to restore the balance, to think of our self-interest, to seek reassurance, etc. Weil speaks of the ego's natural tendency to expand as much as circumstances will permit. This tendency is the opposite of, and in conflict with, a commitment to goodness, which demands self-renunciation.

Weil denies that God is an object and identifies Him with goodness or 'the good', as she puts it. Goodness or God thus lie on the other side of the natural. Weil often uses the word 'supernatural', meaning that one can only reach it by transcending the natural in one and turning one's back on 'the worldly' – on the demands of the marketplace, for example, by turning away from the wilfulness needed to advance in politics, etc. Here, one abandons the ego in order to find one's soul, to enter into spiritual life.

But now you may ask: what has all this to do with sexual or romantic love? The answer is that sexual love could be worldly; indeed, it often begins that way, and may well remain there. In the light of what I said above, it is not surprising that this should be so. But sexuality as such, however earthly, does not exclude spirituality. Indeed, I think we need to distinguish – as Plato does in the *Phaedo* – between the worldly and the otherworldly. As I pointed out in my book on the *Phaedo*: 'For Socrates, from the start, human beings are flesh-and-blood beings interacting with one another in a public life. It is within such a life that the possibilities of good and evil are to be found.'[35] In that book, I was contrasting Plato's Socrates with René Descartes.[36] Thus, for Socrates in the *Phaedo* there is nothing wrong with either sexuality and sexual pleasures as such, or with the pleasures of food. It is when these pleasures are contaminated with the ego, as when romantic love becomes possessive, obsessive or uncaring, or when the desire for food turns into gluttony, that we are distanced from the goodness and the spiritual aspects of life. I now turn to another question that Nozick raises. He writes:

> To be englowed by someone's love, it must be we ourselves who are loved, not a whitewashed version of ourselves, not just a portion. In the complete intimacy of love, a partner knows us as we are, fully. It is no reassurance to be loved by someone ignorant of those traits and features we feel might make us unlovable . . . In the full intimacy of love, the full person is known and cleansed and accepted. And healed.[37]

I would add: provided he or she remains open to the other and does not hide. Further on, Nozick writes:

> You can fall in love with someone because of certain characteristics and you can continue to delight in these; but eventually you must

love the person himself, and not for the characteristics, not, at any rate, for any delimited list of them. But what does this mean, exactly?[38]

Nozick continues:

Characteristics must have played some important role, for otherwise why was not a different person loved just as well? Yet if we continue to be loved 'for' the characteristics, then the love seems conditional, something that might change or disappear if the characteristics do.[39]

Yes, very true. Nozick goes on:

With people [as opposed to ducklings], perhaps characteristics set off the imprint of love, but then the person is loved in a way that is no longer based upon retaining those characteristics. This will be helped if the love is based at first upon a wide range of characteristics; it begins as conditional, contingent upon the loved person's having these desirable characteristics, yet given their range and tenacity, it is not insecure.[40]

In a footnote, Nozick adds: 'Being loved *for* characteristics seems to go with the notion of love being deserved, the characteristics being the basis of the desert. This notion of love's being deserved is a strange one.' Hence, 'to be worthy of (romantic) love, then, is simply to have the capacity to love in return.'[41]

At this point, Nozick turns to practical considerations: 'Once you have come to know a person well, it would take a large investment of time and energy to reach the comparable point with another person, so there is a barrier to switching . . .'[42] This may be true, but it is at least partly self-regarding. I think Nozick is nearer the mark when he refers to 'commitment to a particular person'.[43] If I may briefly develop this in my own way: when one enters into a friendship or love relationship with another person, one finds the other in the way they respond to one. In these responses and in one's own responses to them, each person comes alive to the other and becomes an individual – an individual in the reciprocity and the network of communications that emerge. Here, each is in contact with the other, hopefully open to the other, and concerned for the other. The two-way relationship thus established is a moral one: two people are thus bound together by bonds of loyalty and trust. In such a relationship the characteristics of the other fade into insignificance.

Moreover, a common life in time also forms a common past, common memories, and common experiences. That is how the two individuals come to be bound to each other as individuals. This, in short, is my answer to what it means to come to love another person for himself or herself and not for his or her characteristics and qualities. Such an attachment does not have to be egocentric or narcissistic, or a mutual protection society for two. It can allow spaces in people's togetherness, and let the winds of heaven dance between them.

Nozick returns to the formation of a *we* in a love relationship: 'The intention in love is to form a *we* and to identify with it as an extended self.'[44] I do not find this notion particularly enlightening. All I will say is that one normally enters into a romantic love relationship spontaneously and, hopefully, without any hidden agenda. One has to weather various storms and work at the relationship, and if one is honest and lucky, one may get somewhere in that relationship.

I do not find anything of further interest in what Nozick has to say in the remainder of this chapter, so I shall turn to the next chapter (on emotions). Having done so, I shall have to take a rain-check, because again I find it of very little interest.

III

I said that the contents of the first nine chapters of Nozick's book are scattered. This is not true of the material presented in Chapters 10–18. I would describe the first nine chapters of the book as 'decent' and am sorry that I cannot be more enthusiastic than that. In the next nine chapters, too, Nozick tries to say something he believes to be important; unfortunately – and it gives me no pleasure to say this – he fails to do so.

Nozick begins Chapter 10 (on happiness) by asking whether 'happiness is the *only* important thing about life; all that should matter to a person (as some theorists have claimed)'.[45] He speaks of the 'openness of happiness, its generosity of spirit and width of appreciation', and notes that this characterization 'gets warped and constricted by the claim that only happiness matters'.[46]

Nozick approaches the question whether happiness is the *only* or the *most* important thing in life by trying to separate 'pleasure or happiness' from a concern for significances that bestow meaning on life and lend depth to a person's feelings. 'We are not empty containers or buckets', he writes, 'to be stuffed with good things.'[47] Perhaps Nozick should have said 'goodies'. He is thinking of people with no 'inner lives'.[48] Further on, he writes: 'We care about things in addition to how our lives *feel* to us from the inside'.[49]

This is followed by a thought experiment: 'Imagine a machine that could give you any experience (or sequence of experiences) you might desire'.[50] Nozick goes on: 'You can live your fondest dreams "from the inside". Would you choose to do this for the rest of your life? If not, why not?'[51]

I do understand the question that Nozick wishes to investigate here, but I am sceptical about the conceptual presupposition of the framework within which he wants to do so. What is this 'living your fondest dreams from the inside'? We form our fondest dreams in the course of a life shared with others. And what comes next . . .? In this connection, we can imagine a variety of different scenarios. On the one hand, there are people who, for whatever reason, cannot enter such a communal life and, within it, build up a life of their own; on the other, there are those who come to be alienated from that life. Some turn into drug addicts, others become catatonic. Less extremely, there are people who make their life an imitation; they follow the latest fashions, for instance, or become totally conventional in their morality. The possibilities are numerous.

What comes closest to Nozick's imaginary scenario of 'living your fondest dreams from the inside'? I suppose we are talking about a person with a lively imagination who, for one reason or another, is deeply disappointed with his life and withdraws into himself. He may, of course, be creative and find some happiness in his own company and the work he is doing – he may be some sort of Proust, writing about his disappointing life and its lost possibilities. Or he may uncreatively wallow in his disappointment and waste his life. A wasted life, in this sense, is of course an unhappy life. There is no simple and easy distinction against whose background Nozick's question could be answered. I would like to give my own answer to this question in the form of a quote from my book *Raskolnikov's Rebirth: Psychology and the Understanding of Good and Evil*:

> For a man to be happy there must not only be things for him to be glad about and enjoy, he must also have the capacity to be glad and to enjoy things. He must be able to take an interest in people, to find pleasure in things, to be able to forgive those who hurt him, to feel grateful for what he has. This is something that comes from *him*. So the sources of whatever happiness one finds in life also lie within one. If a person didn't care for people, was not interested in anything, did not appreciate the good things in life, if he didn't find some things good, neither could make him happy. If he was full of resentment, or he turned up his nose at everything, or if he had no interests and

were indifferent to what goes on around him, he could find no happiness in life.

Someone who, at an extreme, takes an interest in nothing but himself, who doesn't care for others, who feels no affection for anyone and forms no attachments, cannot find happiness. Such a person, it is true, would be incapable of deep pain either. But it would be the emptiness of his life that is the source of his unhappiness. He might run after one momentary pleasure or another and describe himself as 'looking for happiness'. But he would be looking for it in the wrong place. For as he is unable to stop anywhere and grow roots the only thing he can find are 'sensations'. He may seek to obtain power, if he is that way inclined, in the hope that it will compensate for his inner poverty. Often that will lead him to evil, to harm others and bring pain into their lives.

Thus if a man is unable to find beauty in things, if he values nothing, if he lacks the capacity for gratitude, nothing will make him happy. For instance, if he believes that everything can be bought, if he measures the worth of things in terms of money, if he sees no intrinsic worth or beauty in them, something that inheres in them quite apart from their utility, or what they would bring him as possessions, nothing can make such a person happy. His life would exclude those forms of significance in relation to which he could find most of the things that bring happiness – fullness of life, gratitude, appreciation, spiritual nourishment. Such a person would say that he was happy while he was able to satisfy his desires and lusts. But what inner life can we attribute to him would be like quicksand: nothing would take there. He is like a man who stuffs himself with food which gives him neither nourishment nor satiety. Socrates describes him in the *Gorgias* as a man who tries to fill a leaking vessel using a sieve.[52]

Nozick writes: 'The vow that only happiness matters ignores the question of what *we* – the very ones to be happy – are like. How could the most important thing about life be what it *contains*?'[53] He continues:

A person who wants to write a poem needn't want (primarily) the felt qualities of writing or the felt qualities of being known to have written a poem. He may want, primarily, *to write* such a poem – for example, because he thinks *it* is valuable, or the activity of doing so is, with no special focus upon any felt qualities.[54]

Nozick sums the matter up as follows: 'We care about things in addition to how our lives *feel* to us from the inside'.[55] I find it difficult to make sense of the distinction that Nozick draws in setting up his thought experiment. He speaks of 'what life *contains*'. Fine; one can say that someone's life *contains* happiness, or pain, or pleasure. In other words, there is much in his life that makes him happy or gives him pain. How could this leave out what he and what his life is like? What is it to want to write a poem primarily for the felt qualities of writing? The closest case I can imagine here is that of someone who likes to *pretend* that he is writing a poem, who plays at being a poet. Writing a poem and playing at being a poet by pretending to write a poem are two different *activities* – except that actually writing a poem is the primary activity that the pretence apes. The latter is not something *inside*, something interior. Rather, what we have here are different activities, and whether we find happiness in them depends on what we do and on how things go.

A child may find happiness in playing games; she may, indeed, be imaginative and creative in the games she plays. A child or an adult may be unable to find happiness because many of his activities are *copies* – they do not engage him creatively, he does not give anything of himself in what he is doing, perhaps because he has nothing to give. As I said, our happiness depends on *both*, our capacities (on what we are like) and external circumstances. Moreover, one person may have the capacity to find happiness in circumstances in which most others would complain.

What Nozick is trying to capture cannot, I think, be captured in the way he tries to do: 'the felt experiences of pleasure and happiness' *versus* 'what we ourselves are like'. It is true that there are people who, to varying degrees, are out of touch with reality and live in a fantasy world. One example would be the kind of narcissistic woman portrayed in the film *Sunset Boulevard* – one who is growing old and losing her looks, together with the contentment derived from other people's admiration. *As a person*, she is the same as when she was young, except that her external circumstances have radically changed, and she lacks the capacity to adjust to this change. It is her narcissism that stands in the way. She pretends to have adapted, but – unsurprisingly – the strategy does not work.

Nozick says: 'We care about more than just how things feel to us from the inside; there is more to life than feeling happy.'[56] Yes, of course, there is more to life than feeling happy. But is this just a matter of how things feel to us from the inside? The ageing actress, Gloria Swanson, in *Sunset Boulevard* would rather pretend, though she does not succeed. But it is because she would rather pretend, because she cannot accept reality, that she cannot find happiness in her old age, the way many others do. The trouble with her is that she thinks too much about herself, is too much wrapped up in herself. That is what lies at the centre of her trouble: she is wrapped up in herself – this is her narcissism – and thinks too much about being happy. Let me quote a few more lines from *Raskolnikov's Rebirth*:

> Generally, engrossed in the activities to which they give themselves they [people] think little about their happiness and care little about the dangers and discomfort to which those activities may expose them. The fact that they are behind their actions, that they put up with pain and discomfort willingly, does not mean that they do so for the sake of the reward in which they will find happiness. To say that 'men want to be happy' in this qualified sense is one thing, to say that they want the different things they seek as a means to happiness is quite another thing. In fact, happiness is something that always eludes those who seek it directly: understandably, since it has no substance of its own. It is not something over and above the different things in which men find happiness. The moment any one of them is made into a *means* to happiness it can no longer bring happiness . . . A person will find happiness, I am inclined to say, if he can do whatever he does creatively, or in other words, by giving himself to it. But, of course, one has to add: if he is lucky, or other things permitting.[57]

Nozick writes: 'My reflections about happiness thus far have been about the *limits* of its role in life. What *is* its proper role, though, and what exactly is happiness; why has its role so often been exaggerated?'[58] In other words: Is happiness the satisfaction one obtains when one's desires are satisfied? Or is it the capacity to be pleased with what one has and to enjoy what one does? Is the happy person one who enjoys life, or one who has attained inner peace? Or is the attainment of inner peace a condition of being able to give oneself to life? So, how far does a person's happiness depend on his state of soul, his values and attitudes to things, and what role do his external circumstances play in this? And if I may add a further question, which I am not sure Nozick has discussed: Can the desire for happiness be anything other than a form of self-seeking? Nozick's discussion of these questions extends over the rest of his book and, apart from a few lucid moments, becomes increasingly remote and abstract.

First, Nozick distinguishes between three types of happiness: (i) being happy at some event, such as finally having succeeded at something for which one had been working hard, or that something good has happened to someone whom one cares for and loves; (ii) 'feeling that your life is good now', the attainment of something that makes a difference to your life as a whole for good;[59] (iii) 'satisfaction with one's life as a whole'.[60] Nozick concludes the chapter by noting that 'we have found various reasons for thinking that happiness is not the only important thing in life.' He adds: 'Nevertheless I want to recall . . . how undeniably wonderful happiness, and a happy disposition can be. How natural then that sometimes we think happiness is the most important thing in life'.[61]

The next chapter ('Focus') starts with the words: 'Emotions are to be connected to actuality.'[62] I have already said that I find very little to discuss in Nozick's chapter on the emotions. For example, commenting on recent philosophical discussions of the subject, he writes: 'Emotions, these philosophers say, have a common structure of three components: a belief, an evaluation, and a feeling'.[63] I prefer to say that emotions are our responses to things, events, and situations, and that we perceive or grasp the character of what we thus respond to, affectively. It is, to a considerable extent, through our emotions that we keep in touch with life and our surroundings. A person who, in his development, moves towards greater unity of self and autonomy, is someone whose reason and emotions have attained some integration. However, to be in touch with life and one's surroundings one has to be open to one's emotions – to pain, among other things. This takes courage, resilience and love.

At the beginning of the chapter, Nozick speaks of our response to traumas experienced by those we love and to monstrous public evil, noting that our emotions of sadness, sorrow, and horror 'will conflict with a desire for happiness'.[64] I find this a strange way of putting the point. I don't believe that a person in this situation will think of his happiness or have a desire for it. While I understand what Nozick is trying to get at, his language strikes me as strange: I don't like saying this, but I think it has been corrupted by philosophy. Be that as it may, Nozick draws a helpful distinction, illustrated by an example. There are times, he says, when it might be appropriate to think of preserving oneself, and when there would be nothing selfish about the thought: 'A person in a Nazi extermination camp might focus eventually upon memories of Mozart's music in order to escape the horrors around him'.[65] I would not call this escapism. 'But', so Nozick rightly continues,

> if this were his preoccupation from the beginning, smiling constantly in fond memory of the music, that reaction would be bizarre. Then he would be disconnected from important features of his world, not giving them emotional attention commensurate with the evil they inflict.[66]

Nozick goes on: 'We need an additional reality principle, concerning not the accuracy of attention's focus – the second principle handled this – but its *direction*'.[67] I would say that what we need is experience and common sense. Of course, people may disagree, and people's different psychologies may interfere with finding the right kind of balance. You cannot legislate about these matters with principles – 'reality principles'. Nozick says that 'the fundamental evaluative activity is selectivity of focus, focusing here rather than there'.[68] This is why this chapter is entitled 'Focus'. But I repeat: what we need here is 'judgement', rather than 'principle'. Nozick goes on: 'The example of the experience machine shows we do not want to be disconnected from actuality; we do not want zero percent contact.'[69] Quite honestly, we do not need the example of the experience machine to see that 'we do not want to be disconnected from actuality'.

Strangely enough, Nozick now turns to a consideration of advertising and its manipulation of images.[70] He is thinking, he says, about the way 'attention can be focused upon different parts of actuality', about how 'we might contemplate a reality principle *slanted* toward focus upon the positive insofar as this is possible without significant detachment from the actuality one is amid'.[71] Nozick writes of advertising: 'This mode of creating and utilizing illusion need not come into conflict with the reality principles if the person remains aware it is an induced role.'[72]

I am afraid I don't have a single good word to say about advertising – it generally appeals to the egos of those who take notice of it, so as to promote the commercial interests of those who manufacture and sell the products it promotes. In my book on the *Gorgias*, I used the example of advertising to illustrate what Socrates called 'sophistry' and 'pandering' in that dialogue.[73] I will quote a few lines of what I say there; they are diametrically opposed to what Nozick writes in *The Examined Life*:

You tell people what they would like to hear as opposed to the truth. You appeal to their desire for ease and comfort. You thus reinforce their sense of dependence instead of involving them in any form of activity which requires effort and initiative. You flatter their vanity and thus increase their desire for anything that provides self-gratification. In this way you make them easy to manipulate, incapable of seeking the truth and standing by it. You please them insofar as they like comfort and you give them the easy thing. But you don't give them what is good for them: dignity, independence, responsibility. You do not give them anything that would awake spiritual hunger in them. Instead you deceive them; you make them believe that the transitory pleasures you offer them are good. You dazzle them with these and blind them to other possibilities. All this suits you. For you do not want people to think for themselves, to become self-reliant, to forego pleasure and endure hardship for what they believe. If they did, you could not manipulate them easily.[74]

Let me summarize the steps of Nozick's argument as follows:

(i)   Advertising is an interesting case to consider. Besides its functions of giving information and catching attention and its less happy one of sidestepping rational evaluation, advertising can manipulate images to differentiate a product . . .[75]

(ii) Armed thus with the right cigarette or car or drink, we can play at being a certain way or more easily imagine we are that way. (Even when products do differ, part of their qualities' function might be to fit into and prompt further fantasies.) Sometimes when we behave thus, others will produce fitting responses and thereby make our role more comfortable, even eventually, more authentic. This mode of creating and utilizing illusion need not come into conflict with the reality principles if the person remains aware it is an induced role.[76]

(iii) The ability and opportunity to focus our attention, to choose what we will pay attention to, is an important component of our autonomy. Voluntary control over our attention also is an important feature of our psychological well-being . . . Without such control of the mode and object of our attention, it would be difficult to behave effectively or to have a rounded emotional life.[77]

(iv) Emotions, therefore, do not, or need not, simply wash over us. We can have a certain control over them by modifying the beliefs we hold, through rational criticism or further thought. Philosophy can have a quite practical impact on our emotional lives by providing us with the operative principles of rational belief and evaluation.[78]

I do not want to be unfair, but what is being advocated here seems best described as 'the rational control of the emotions, where possible, even if this involves self-manipulation', with the idea of making life more pleasant, or at least more bearable. What is needed, however, is not the control of emotions, let alone self-manipulation, but the integration of our emotions with our reason. Only then will they be transformed; only by facing them will we have a chance to grow. For example, someone who keeps a grudge may repress his resentment. That grudge will then remain with him, fester, and colour his life. If, on the other hand, he can bring himself to face his resentment, this may eventually lead to his forgiving the person whose actions and attitude towards him he resents. I am, of course, over-simplifying here.

With his rational approach and different principles, Nozick seeks to produce a safe and orderly world. But his approach and language strike me as completely false or artificial. Here is another example of what I mean:

> Someone is said to be 'philosophical' about something where he avoids negative emotions by displacing or diminishing negative evaluations, either by taking the very widest perspective or by selective focus of attention upon facts. Sometimes, though, philosophy – or the third reality principle, at any rate – tells us to focus *upon* the negative. The conflict between this reality principle and our desire to avoid intensely unpleasant feelings may be less severe than it appears. That principle sometimes mandates negative emotions; however, the feelings that form part of negative emotions, while they cannot be pleasant, need not themselves be unpleasant . . .[79]

If someone one loves is severely ill and his or her life is under threat, one would be very worried, concerned, and frightened. Who would describe this as a negative emotion? Would it occur to one to focus on the tone of one's turmoil? Would one describe it as unpleasant? If someone in this situation did so describe it, would we not think that he was very self-centred? Yet this is the language Nozick uses throughout this chapter:

> Sadness in life, unlike sadness in the theatre, *feels* unpleasant, and this truly is a difference in how the experiences feel, in their phenomenology, and is not simply constituted by the different contexts . . . When certain facts or events in life make us unhappy, this is not simply the absence of happiness, but an existing emotion with its own accompanying feeling: sad, flat, depressed. Wouldn't it be best not to feel *these* feelings when we respond with emotion to the facts we evaluate negatively?[80]

The paragraph ends with an equally strange question: 'Is unhappiness necessary as an appropriate response to certain negative facts?'[81] What a strange way to think about emotions and the way they keep us in touch with reality! If our judgements or evaluations were detached from emotional responses, would we not be robots? Nozick appreciates this:

> We want to love some people, and hence to be someone whose own well-being is linked with theirs. When they are worse off, it is

not enough simply to make a dispassionate negative evaluation of ourselves as worse off too, for in what way *are* we worse off then? . . . The emotion of unhappiness we feel is what makes us worse off when they are; it constitutes the way we are worse off and links our well-being directly with theirs.[82]

I'm glad I'm able to agree. Nozick's next paragraph ends with the following question: 'So why do we want to be so constituted as beings who are made *unhappy* over our own situation – wouldn't different strong emotions connect us sufficiently yet be more desirable?'[83] He continues:

In your own case, toward your own suffering, you might strive to win through to the attitude of a theatre audience, whose emotions are felt deeply but not felt as painful. (We have already seen that this would not do towards people one loves. With them, we do not merely feel deeply in some way or other, we are pained by their pain. Not to do this is not to be connected to them in the bond of love.) Yet these deep feelings while not leaving one completely detached from events, leave one a spectator.[84]

Let me interrupt the quotation here, to say that while a theatre spectator's responses to what goes on in a play may be imaginative, I would not wish to speak of them as deep. To go back to the passage I was quoting: 'Perhaps your feeling unhappy (or happy) at certain events is what makes these events part of *your* life.'[85] But if this were so, what about the case where we feel unhappy or happy about certain events in the life of someone we love? In any case, if we lived our lives as spectators of their events, we would again lose touch with reality – as in the case of being a spectator to events in other people's lives.

At the end of the chapter, Nozick asks: 'Why do we want to live our lives, rather than be spectators to them?'[86] He answers: 'Perhaps actual unhappiness or happiness is what makes our lives serious – not just a play or game.'[87] I agree. Nozick then asks: 'But why do we want our lives to be serious?' His reply, as I understand it, is that a life which is a game is a shallow life.

The next chapter (Chapter 12, 'Being More Real') begins well: 'Part of the self's value dwells in its ability to transform *itself* and so be (to a considerable extent) self-creating'.[88] As I would put it: 'The self participates in its own development.' Nozick then asks: 'When do you feel most real?'[89] He says, rightly, that being real is not the same thing as existing. Nozick explains that when we speak of a person as real, we mean that he is 'vivid, concentrated, focused, delineated, integrated, inwardly beautiful'.[90] Let me note that when we say that a person is said to be real, we mean that he is 'there', has 'presence'. Here, Nozick and I are in agreement. He observes that people say, for example, that 'they feel most real when they feel most creative'.[91] They feel most real, in other words, when they give of themselves, when they engage with something they care about or are interested in.

Nozick now raises another question: 'When do you feel most yourself?' Here, I disagree with his claim that the two questions are very close. If you are not genuine, you are not yourself. Not much further along in the text, Nozick repeats what he said earlier, viz. what has reality is not the same as what exists. Perhaps 'reality', understood in the relevant sense, has several antitheses. Above, I said that 'real' (in this sense) means 'being there'. Its antithesis is 'being withdrawn'. Again, the opposite of being withdrawn is 'being in contact', 'being engaged'. I said earlier that we are in contact with others through our affective responses; it is in those responses that we are there. 'Not being yourself', 'not being genuine', is another antithesis of being real.

This is pretty much what Nozick has to say in the chapter. However, it contains some diversions and, if I may put it that way, some 'unreality' – for instance, what he says about how to assess the *overall* reality of the self and the 'reality curve'.[92] If I understand them rightly, Nozick's comments on people who feel their own reality enhanced in the presence of celebrities, are, to put it politely, not very enlightening. People may feel that the presence of celebrities enhances their own reality, but this is an illusion and a matter of self-deception. 'But why', Nozick asks, 'doesn't it [the general public] cry out that the clothes contain no emperor?'[93] The answer is: because it is the public's adulation that has turned certain people into celebrities.

I shall pass over the rest of Nozick's Chapter 12 in silence; nor do I find much to discuss in the following chapter (Chapter 13, 'Selflessness') and will therefore ignore it. However, I would like to draw attention to a distinction of which Nozick seems to be unaware. The term 'self' has developed out of the use of the reflexive pronoun – e.g. 'He did it to himself', 'He has not been himself today' – and may mean 'his usual self'. Another example would be 'self-knowledge'. Thus, we also speak of someone who has 'come to himself' or 'found himself', or who 'is himself'. Then again, we speak of someone as 'selfish', 'self-interested', or 'self-centred'. Hence, there is no contradiction in saying that, in order to come to yourself, or find yourself, you have 'to turn away from yourself', 'renounce yourself', or 'forget yourself'. Thus, a selfless person is not a 'blank' person, one who has no personality or lacks reality. In fact, the opposite is the case. One further note, which will be relevant to some of the later chapters in Nozick's book: if you aim at selflessness in order to avoid or lessen the woes of this world, you will never find selflessness, for it is for the sake of the self – the ego – that you are seeking it. In this connection, I would like to quote another paragraph from the chapter on selflessness and then comment on it:

> Some Eastern theories condemn the self on three counts: First, the self interferes with our experiencing the deepest reality, and also with experiencing things in general as they are; second, it makes us unhappy or it interferes with our having the highest happiness; third, the self is not our full reality, yet we mistakenly believe it is.[94]

Now, I do not know these 'Eastern theories' or 'philosophies', but I understand what is being said here. (i) I agree that a person who is preoccupied with himself will not be open to the pain of others; his sympathy and compassion will be superficial and limited, and he will have little commerce with the pain and suffering that are important aspects of the weave of life. (ii) I suppose that by 'the highest happiness' is meant a point where we are thoroughly absorbed in what we value and give ourselves to it. We may, of course, encounter troubles and difficulties, but then we also experience the peace that comes with our devotion. However, a word of caution: our devotion must be genuine, pure, devoid of all ulterior motives that would allow the self to enter through the back door. (iii) Yes, most people are – to some extent at least – self-orientated, and they believe the self to be their full reality, whether they defend themselves when attacked, or feel low when humiliated. A more extreme example would be the case of a person who despairs over the feeling that he is nothing. But a person who has found genuine humility will not experience the sting of humiliation, of being ignored, etc.

In my view, Nozick's next chapter ('Stances') is a real muddle. It begins by delineating three life-stances: egoistic, relational, and absolute. 'Later', Nozick tells us, 'we consider a fourth that might integrate these'.[95] I won't go into Nozick's explanations of what these stances amount to, but I have a query about the second stance which, Nozick tells us, 'sees the primary location of value in relations or connections, primarily within relations of the self with other things (or other selves)'.[96] To me, this division among relations seems wholly superfluous. In his relation with others, a person is either focused on the self – a narcissist, to take an extreme case – or he is absorbed in what he values and strives to achieve. He may, for example, love and care for someone – his mother or wife, say – in a wholly self-less manner, or his love may be contaminated by the self in a variety of (subtle) ways.

Further along in the chapter, Nozick talks about the egoist:

> To demarcate its self as valuable, not merely to shape desires, the egoistic stance has to transcend its own egoistic orientation . . . I am saying not merely that to deny the importance in others' case would involve him in an inconsistency – someone may not care very much about avoiding inconsistencies – but that he cannot view his own life as having what is important unless he views others in the same light, so that the same standard can give them the same importance.[97]

My reaction is that only a philosopher can talk like that, and so much the worse for him! An egoist is an egoist; he always, consistently, puts himself first. He recognizes that other egoists do the same. Unlike Nozick, he does not use big words – 'I view my own life as having what is important.' He just puts himself first. If you were to say to him, 'How can your life be the most important thing in the world?' he would reply: 'To me it is, for it is my life'. If he were philosophically articulate, he might add: 'It is the same with other people, they take exactly the same attitude towards their lives as I take towards mine. What is important for each person about his life is that it is *his* life.' Let us continue with Nozick: 'The absolutist stance specifies the locus of value as the total of reality in the world; this includes one's own reality and that of one's connections – the egoist's and the relationist concern – as portions, albeit tiny ones'.[98]

To be blunt: this is another piece of philosophical nonsense. First, it is far from clear what 'the locus of value as the total of reality in the world' could mean. The absolutist, as I understand it, believes in or is committed to certain absolute values. He holds, for instance, that every human being or animal on earth is important and that one should not let any harm come to them. Is this incompatible with egoism? Of course it is. Does this mean that one must not take care of oneself when the need arises? Of course not. All it means is that one must not put oneself first and neglect others, put them second.

Nozick asks: can the three stances be reconciled? As I see it, the answer is 'Obviously not'. A little further on, Nozick writes: 'Although acting on the absolutist stance might increase a person's own reality and hence serve the egoist stance without this being the actions' object, still, not all conflict among these two stances can thereby be avoided'.[99] I wish Nozick's language were more down-to-earth. But yes, 'increasing a person's reality', if only *in appearance* – by acquiring more power, for instance – may serve the egoist stance.

On the other hand, if a person gradually learns to forget himself and comes to himself, thereby becoming more real than he was, this would not serve the egoist stance. If, however, he turns away from himself to find greater peace, for example, then he will not have freed himself from the egoist stance – indeed, he will not really have turned away from himself. Still, to explain all this in Nozick's language is of little help, and having to respond to him in that language, however briefly, a personal ordeal. Nozick says: 'While each of the three stances is faulty by itself, each has its appeal . . . and its legitimate claim'.[100] I have already spent too much time on this chapter and do not see what appeal egoism can have – except, at a basic level, to the egoist. Nor do I see what appeal it could have for Nozick, unless he confuses looking after one's own interest – in certain circumstances – with egoism.

As for Hillel's 'If I am not for myself, who will be?', [101] imagine the following situation: We are poor, and I am ill. I reduce my food intake so that we can give our dog a bit more. My wife protests: 'You are ill, I don't want you to lose strength.' Well, here's the answer to Hillel. Nozick writes: 'A life that neglects any one of the factors . . . will be inadequate.'[102] As I said, you cannot talk generally. There are circumstances where it is not egoistic to think of oneself, even to put oneself first. On the other hand, there is a difference between self-renunciation in particular circumstances and trying to be a saint. We are not all saints and, for some people, the attempt to be one in such-and-such circumstances can only result in falsehood.

I now turn to the next chapter of Nozick's book, entitled 'Value and Meaning'. It begins ominously, and I shall explain why I say this:

> The notion of reality has various aspects or dimensions. To be more intense and vivid is to be more real (holding other things equal), to be more valuable is to be more real, and so on. To have a higher score along any one of the various dimensions that make up the notion of reality (holding everything constant) is to be more real.[103]

I said I would explain why I think this passage 'ominous'. I remember from my student days a line from a good film by Cocteau, called, I think, *Les Enfants Terribles*. The line, which I thought very appropriate, was about a young girl's relation to her brother. It went as follows: 'C'est une arraigné et elle fille sa toile' – 'She is a spider and she weaves her web'. In the present case, the web is being woven by a philosopher, and it is he who becomes its captive. Indeed, as Nozick's book progresses, the web becomes increasingly dense. The web in question is the philosopher's language; all simplicity is lost, and the ground is shifting under our feet. At this point, I shall only select two intriguing passages which I do not understand. The first concerns Nozick's remarks about Cartesian dualism:

> Consciousness and the mind not only enable an organism to unify its activities over time; at any given moment, consciousness is tightly unified with physical/biological processes then occurring. What we have, then, is an apparently enormous diversity which is unified to a very high degree – that is, we have an extremely high degree of organic unity, hence something extremely valuable. If (degree of) value is (degree of) organic unity, the mind-body problem shows that people are very valuable. Solving this problem will require understanding how this very high degree of value is possible.[104]

My only comment, in the language of the markets, is: what has this got to do with the price of fish? Nozick continues: 'To value something is to stand in a particular close, positive psychological and attitudinal relation to it, a relation marked by high organic unity'.[105] This still throws no light on the passage I quoted earlier. To value something is to give oneself to it. The relation is one of love and commitment. I have no further comment to make on this chapter. I must confess that the book is now beginning to look more like a metaphysical treatise than a philosophical meditation reaching its climax in Chapter 17 and the appendix on 'The Metaphysics of Reality'. I shall return to these. First, we come to Chapter 16, which is entitled 'Importance and Weight'.

It begins as follows: 'We want to be important in some way, to count in the world and make a difference to it'.[106] I don't know that wanting to be important and wanting to make a difference to the world are the same thing. Wanting to be important is wanting one's ego to expand, whereas genuinely wanting to make a difference to the world is caring to do some good in it, wanting to make a contribution to its betterment – in other words, giving something of oneself, not taking something for oneself.

Nozick next turns to the game of chess. He says that 'given the immense amount of intellectual power and energy it takes', one gets disproportionately little out of it.[107] One gets pleasure out of it; but it is a game, and as such it doesn't deepen the players. I do not understand why Nozick finds it 'most desirable to have value and importance together', [108] when under 'importance' he includes 'material wealth and power as forms of it'.[109] Given what he says about importance – 'having external impact or effect', 'counting', 'simply being paid attention to is something we want' – I cannot see any connection between importance and value. If it were a matter of valuing something and attaching importance to it, I would understand. But I do not see that all the heavy weather this chapter makes about importance has anything to do with value.

I agree with what Nozick says a few pages further along, without being clear about how this chapter hangs together. Thus, Nozick writes: 'If a philosopher tells us that he thinks for the money, a doctor that she cures illness for it . . . then we feel their activity is somehow soiled.'[110] I entirely agree. In the next paragraph, he asks: 'If importance is indeed a dimension of reality, must we then say that merely possessing power does give one greater reality?'[111] He continues: 'It is because importance was defined neutrally . . . that we have been forced through these thickets of reasons to show the obvious: that certain modes of such importance do not make someone more real'.[112] Yes, but that is really no excuse for the 'thickets of reasons'.

Is an important doctor more real than one who is not? I once met a doctor who was considered the best in his field. He was important, and how he knew it: he was full of himself. Did that make him real? On the contrary, it stood in the way of his being real. Why? Because everything he did was filtered through his inflated ego, so as to increase that inflation. The doctor had come to the hospital where my father was unconscious – with a blood clot in his brain – to give him a lumbar puncture. When I approached him about the result, he was so full of himself that he ignored me: he had done what he had come for, and the report would be submitted to the hospital. My father died that night in hospital, and I never set eyes on this famous doctor again. Real? No, he was on a perpetual ego-trip.

Nozick's chapter on 'Importance and Weight' now turns to weight: 'A weighty person is not blown by winds of fashion or scrutiny. The Romans called it *gravitas*'.[113] Weight, Nozick says, is an equilibrium notion. However, I must point out that this covers a range of different conditions. We have, at one end of the spectrum, a person whose solidity is a form of rigidity. His position in society is such that everyone looks up at him; he has a position to maintain and won't be blown by the winds of fashion. But, as Kafka puts it in his *Diaries*,

whoever appears as a complete citizen, that is, travels over the sea in a ship with foam before him and wake behind, that is, with much effect round about, quite different from the man in the waves on a few planks of wood that even bump against and submerge each other – he, this gentleman and citizen, is in no lesser danger. For he and his

property are not one, but two, and whoever destroys the connection
destroys him at the same time.[114]

We have to contrast such a person with someone who has *found* himself,
someone who *is* himself. He won't be blown by winds of fashion or
scrutiny. He is himself, in that he has made his values and properties
his own; he and his properties are one, not two. He does not need to
bolster himself up; he is modest. If his words have weight, this weight
is invisible to him. What strikes us about him is not his weight but his
humility.

Towards the end of this chapter, Nozick writes: 'This simple picture of
these four evaluative dimensions of reality – value, meaning, importance
and weight – places them in illuminating and satisfying relationship'.[115]
Here, I am simply dumbstruck. You will see why, when we turn to the
next chapter in Nozick's book, with its multiple dimensions and polyhe-
drons of reality. In the current chapter, Nozick writes: 'Unfortunately for
theoretical purposes, however, – but perhaps fortunately for life – these
four do not exhaust the relevant kinds of evaluations we want to make'.[116]
In the chapter's final paragraph, we read:

> It is not surprising that we have encountered a plethora of evaluative
> dimensions, an explosion. The growing list of evaluative dimensions
> simply lists the dimensions of reality. These are the dimensions that
> make something more real.[117]

This inconspicuous word 'something' hides a great deal – could the
'something' be anything? – and plunges us into the sea of metaphysics: if
we are not already there, that is.

I now turn to Chapter 13, 'The Matrix of Reality':

> In the previous meditation we expanded the list of dimensions of
> reality from the initial four – value, meaning, importance and weight
> – to include many others as well. Let us consider the widest possible
> list of relevant dimensions. It contains . . .[118]

At this point, readers of Nozick will have to take a deep breath: I counted
54 of these dimensions. A few pages into the chapter, Nozick tells us:

> The remainder of this section, I admit, contains strange and some-
> times bewildering pieces of theorizing, very much against the grain
> of contemporary philosophy. Omitting it would save me much grief

from the current philosophical community – writing it has already cost me uneasiness.[119]

I do not now count myself as belonging to the current philosophical community, but I have a sense of what Nozick is trying to say. I will later try to put the matter concisely and in my own way. It seems to me that Nozick has allowed himself to get lost in a sea of words. When I was a research student in London, I spent about a year and a half working in the Turkish section of the British Broadcasting Corporation. Every few months, we received a large envelope with an equally large chart and some 15 or 20 pages of explanation from someone who, I imagine, was a philosopher *manqué*. The chart was so elaborate, so thorough, that we used to stick it on our notice board, tie the explanatory pages together with a string, and let them hang beneath the board. The man who had devised the chart was clearly intelligent and punctilious, but his hold on reality was somewhat tenuous. Nozick's chapter on 'The Matrix of Reality' and some of the material that precedes and follows it, reminds me of those charts and their attendant explanations.

To my surprise, Nozick eventually emerges from his sea of words with a reference to J. L. Austin's discussion of the use of the word 'real' in *Sense and Sensibilia*. While this is timely, Nozick devotes only one (long) paragraph to it and then completely forgets about it, nor does it make any difference to the further development of his argument. Nozick provides quite a good, short summary of what Austin says and then concludes: 'That returns us to the task of considering the nature of reality . . . We can agree with Austin, though, that there are many different ways of being more or less real'.[120] Nozick then continues:

> I do hope that the reader has felt (as I have) that grouping these dimensions [value, meaning, weight, importance, intensity, etc.] of reality illuminates both them and the nature of reality. Moreover, arranging the dimensions in the intricate interlacing of the (two-dimensional) chart does not leave them a disconnected list . . . Why else would they fit together that well.[121]

We are now close to the end of 'The Matrix of Reality', I am glad to say. I will not comment on the Appendix to Nozick's book ('The Metaphysics of Reality') but instead express –simply and in my own words – what I suppose Nozick is trying to say. First, let us remember that he was speaking of *a person's* reality. I described this as a person's *thereness*, his 'presence'. Nozick also speaks of the reality a person may be in touch with or fail

to make contact with. We may say that he is in touch with his surroundings, with what goes on around him when understood in terms of life in
general. Nozick does not distinguish between these at all. He talks about
a person finding reality through 'value and meaning, goodness and holiness', as well as through the kind of immortality associated with power,
money, and self-importance. Nozick throws all this into one and the same
basket.[122]

Let me point out, first, that it is through compassion, love and openness – all of which involve forgetting oneself – that one enhances one's
contact with reality. This includes contact with the pleasure, good fortune
and pain of loved ones, the misery of others, and the evil in the world.
One doesn't seek any of this; it is one's love and compassion that put one
in touch with it.

Secondly, I repeat that a *person's* reality and reality in the sense of what
life contains (the warp and the woof of life) are two different things.
Nozick completely fails to distinguish between them. It is by engagement
with our surroundings and with others, through taking a genuine interest in things outside us and caring about others that we *come to ourselves*
or *find our reality*. In being self-protective or defensive (in the Freudian
sense), seeking to compensate for our weaknesses, trying to get our own
back on others, nursing grudges, thinking of our self-interest in what we
do, seeking to boost our own importance, we *fail* to come to ourselves.
We become restricted, confined, and considerably narrow in our give-
and-take with other people. Our interactions are curbed by our ulterior
motives. Our psychological wounds, needs, defences, and commitments,
in the (Freudian) sense of 'unconscious determination' or 'repetition
compulsions', constrict our contacts with others. Our interactions have
only one direction: we are not interested in giving, merely in feathering
our psychological nest. We don't respond to the friendship others show
us; we take it and use it to our psychological advantage.

The result: we solidify and gradually become an empty shell or someone who is motivated by the desire to take and to use. In the latter case, we
may think we are prospering, but inwardly we are impoverished – i.e. we
have less and less to give. While our ego is nourished, we wither away as
a person to whom others can respond positively. Outwardly, we may be
very 'busy' (in Kierkegaard's sense) and there may be lots of people orbit-
ing around us. But inwardly, we are lonely. We may drown that loneliness
in external business, but whatever we make of it, there is little we receive
in return – except at the level of the ego.

So, our life becomes something engineered; it has no inner depth,
receives no spiritual food to foster our growth. Inwardly, we remain

stunted and surrounded by, or entrapped in, a spider's web of deception. That web becomes the substance of our life. Contrast this way of talking with how Nozick expresses himself: the general words and abstractions float in the air; they do not connect with anything.

In the next chapter ('Darkness and Light'), Nozick begins by saying that reality is not wholly rosy, adding that one's sense of reality can be heightened in ways that are either painful or immoral.[123] Nozick refers to this as 'the negative path'. He says that 'someone's route to greatest reality might be a negative one'.[124] In this negative path he also includes 'suffering and tragedy'. But this path to 'greatest reality' is very different – radically different – from one that is immoral. Nozick doesn't seem to have made up his mind on the matter. On the one hand, he quotes Nietzsche: 'The more he [a man] aspires to the height and light, the more strongly [like a tree] do his roots strive earthward, downward, into the dark, the deep – into evil'.[125] On the other hand, Nozick writes: 'Evil *qua* evil does not make something more real; value *qua* value does'.[126] Indeed, he emphasizes this and admits that he feels divided over the question. I have already made it clear where I stand on all this.

Further along, Nozick draws a distinction between different 'layers' of ethic: 'the ethic of respect', 'the ethic of responsiveness', 'the ethic of caring or compassion', and 'the ethic of light'.[127] 'To be a vehicle of light', he writes, 'is to be its *impersonal* vehicle.'[128] The differences between the last three 'layers' is not clear to me.

Towards the end of the chapter, Nozick returns to the question whether reality might not be increased by evil, pain, brutal power or mere wealth.[129] But here I do not follow him:

> With such a formalistic theory, the problem arose . . . This led to attempts, somewhat unconvincing, to show how that formalistic theory of reality could point away from dark content. Instead, we can make the row of light – that is, truth, goodness, beauty and holiness – the content of reality, while all the other dimensions of reality increase reality when (and only when) they enfold *this* content . . . Or perhaps, rather than requiring these other dimensions to be filled by the content of light, we can see them in general as increasing reality provided they are not filled with the *opposite* of light; neutral content will serve within them.[130]

What is in question, as I tried to explain, is fairly simple. Let me reiterate: we find ourselves in honest give-and-take relations with others. That is when we turn outwards and stop thinking of ourselves. The reasons which turn us on ourselves are manifold. As our ego expands, we drift further and further away from finding ourselves. Someone with an inflated ego is caught up in something that personally engages him, even if he acts this out in his relationships with others. He is not *there* for them, but is absorbed by a secret agenda. Evil is always responsive to such secret and private agendas. The evil person, as Plato put it, is not his own master; he is ruled by the needs of the ego in him that he serves.

Nozick's abstract language leads to all manner of complications, and by the end of this chapter on 'Darkness and Light' I have lost the thread of his reasoning. I am afraid I will have to skip the next chapter of Nozick's book ('Theological Explanations'). I have read it with some interest, but have no comments to make. Nor do I have anything to say about Nozick's discussion of the Holocaust, though it is clear that he has strong and deep feelings about it.

IV

In the remainder of *The Examined Life*, Nozick takes up the notion of enlightenment, reflects on spiritual teachers and what (and how) we can learn from them, and talks about wisdom and politics. I have already commented on some of Nozick's remarks that I applaud and won't discuss the last few chapters of the book separately.

In the chapter on enlightenment, Nozick tells us that, according to various Eastern traditions, 'the highest goal of human existence is *enlightenment*'.[131] It is, he explains, revelatory of a deeper reality.[132] And what does that mean? You have to combine philosophy with imagination to answer that question, and I'm afraid I do not find that combination in Nozick's book. Instead, we are served such phrases as 'experiences of an infinite pure substance', 'experience of the vibrant void – an experience Buddhists report as deepest', and 'experience of a full and infinite blissful conscious reality'.[133] In a couple of paragraphs further along, Nozick says: 'The self then is experienced differently, no longer wrapped up in the everyday constituents of consciousness or wholly constituted by it. It may be experienced as a witnessing consciousness out of time . . . The self's boundaries are extended or dissolved'.[134] Here, Nozick is straining towards something that makes sense to me. Indeed, I am reminded of a passage from a play by Eugene O'Neill which puts the point well and strikingly – the play being *Long Day's Journey Into Night*. I quoted it in my book on the *Phaedo*, in the chapter on 'The Wheel of Time' – what does it mean to come out of the wheel of time?[135] Here I quote only one notable passage from the text of the play; it concerns the reflections of a character called Edmund:

A calm sea, that time. Only a lazy ground swell and a slow drowsy roll of the ship. The passengers asleep and none of the crew in sight. No sound of man. Black smoke pouring from the funnels behind and beneath me. Dreaming, not keeping a lookout, feeling alone, and above, and apart, watching the dawn creep like a painted dream over the sky and sea which slept together. Then the moment of ecstatic freedom came. The peace, the end of the quest, the last harbour, the joy of belonging to a fulfilment beyond men's lousy, pitiful, greedy fears and hopes and dreams! And several other times in my life, when I was swimming far out, or lying alone on a beach, I have had the same experience. Became the sun, the hot sand, green seaweed anchored to a rock, swaying in the tide. Like a saint's vision of beatitude. Like the veil of things as they seem drawn back by an unseen hand. For a second there is meaning! Then the hand lets the veil fall and you are alone, lost in the fog again, and you stumble on towards nowhere, for no good reason! (*He grins wryly.*) It was a great mistake, my being born a man, I would have been much more successful as a sea-gull or a fish.[136]

It takes imagination and poetry to express this, but also – and especially – freedom from metaphysics. What is at issue here is the way in which time and the self (the ego) blur our vision of life, and what is revealed when we come to be free of them. In fairness, Nozick does here make an effort in the right direction. Towards the end of the chapter, he raises a good question:

The doctrine of enlightenment therefore denies the ultimate reality of tragedy . . . Does that doctrine thereby contain the deepest wisdom, or is it the very highest and most beautiful foolishness? Shouldn't we suspect that enlightenment, and its whole background theory, is too good to be true? . . . Isn't the hard and ultimate wisdom rather this: that there is no escaping the human condition, and the belief that one can, is, in the last analysis, shallow?[137]

If I may put it like this, somewhat humorously: Which would one rather be – a seagull, or perhaps a fish, or a human being? Edmund, in O'Neill's play, is someone inadequate; he finds relief in a genuine glimpse of the eternal. As he puts it: 'It was a great mistake, my being born a man.'[138] Maybe he cannot learn to cope with life; not everyone can. But there are *some* who can. Certainly, I believe that we should learn to live life without softening its pains and blows. That would put us in touch with the deepest spiritual aspect of life. This is what, as I understand it, the great spiritual religions mean to teach us.

I want to finish by saying that if my comments on Nozick have, at times, been harsh and somewhat sweeping, I have, nevertheless, tried to be honest and just. I am sorry if I have misunderstood him. I certainly did not have an axe to grind.

Notes

1 Robert Nozick, *The Examined Life: Philosophical Meditations* (New York: Simon & Schuster, 1990), 12.
2 Ibid., 18.
3 Ibid.
4 Ibid., 301. See also 302.
5 Ibid., 254.
6 Ibid., 303.
7 Ibid., 21.
8 Ibid., 22.
9 Ibid.
10 Ibid., 24.
11 Ibid., 57.
12 Rainer Maria Rilke, *Sonnets to Orpheus*, trans. J. B. Leishman (London: Hogarth Press, 1936), Sonnet XIII.
13 Ibid., Sonnet XV.
14 Nozick, *The Examined Life*, 62.
15 Ibid.
16 Ibid.
17 Ibid., 63.
18 Ibid.
19 Ibid., 64.
20 Ibid.
21 Ibid., 68.
22 Ibid., 69.
23 Ibid., 70.
24 Ibid., 71.
25 Ibid.
26 Ibid.
27 Ibid., 72.
28 Ibid., 74.
29 Ilham Dilman, *Love: Its Forms, Dimensions and Paradoxes* (London: Macmillan, 1998), xv–xvi.
30 Simone Weil, *Waiting for God*, trans. Emma Craufurd (New York: Harper & Row, 1973), 204.
31 This is what I had in mind earlier when I said that love's bond must

not be allowed to be determined by the lovers' psychologies. In my more recent work, I distinguish between a 'determining psychology' and an 'enabling psychology'. See, for example, *The Self, the Soul, and the Psychology of Good and Evil* (London: Routledge, 2005), 84. [Editorial Note: Dilman is here referring to the unpublished manuscript of this book.]

32 Weil, *Waiting for God*, 205.
33 Kahlil Gibran, *The Prophet* (Ware, Herts.: Wordsworth, 1966), 7.
34 Ibid.
35 Ilham Dilman, *Philosophy and the Philosophic Life* (London: Macmillan, 1992), 74.
36 Ibid.
37 Nozick, *The Examined Life*, 74.
38 Ibid.
39 Ibid.
40 Ibid., 75–6.
41 Ibid.
42 Ibid., 77.
43 Ibid.
44 Ibid., 78.
45 Ibid., 99.
46 Ibid., 117.
47 Ibid. 102.
48 Ibid.
49 Ibid., 104.
50 Ibid.
51 Ibid., 104–5.
52 Ilham Dilman, *Raskolnikov's Rebirth: Psychology and the Understanding of Good and Evil* (Chicago, Ill.: Open Court, 2000), 81–82.
53 Nozick, *The Examined Life*, 102.
54 Ibid., 104.
55 Ibid.
56 Ibid.
57 Dilman, *Raskolnikov's Rebirth*, 88.
58 Nozick, *The Examined Life*, 108.
59 Ibid., 108–10.
60 Ibid. I am not sure about the difference between (ii) and (iii).
61 Ibid., 117.
62 Ibid., 118.
63 Ibid., 87.
64 Ibid., 118.

65 Ibid.
66 Ibid., 118–19.
67 Ibid., 119.
68 Ibid., 119–20.
69 Ibid., 120.
70 Ibid., 121.
71 Ibid.
72 Ibid., 122.
73 Ilham Dilman, *Morality and the Inner Life: A Study in Plato's 'Gorgias'* (London: Macmillan, 1979), 22.
74 Ibid.
75 Nozick, *The Examined Life*, 121.
76 Ibid., 122.
77 Ibid.
78 Ibid., 122–3.
79 Ibid., 123.
80 Ibid., 125.
81 Ibid.
82 Ibid., 126.
83 Ibid.
84 Ibid.
85 Ibid.
86 Ibid., 127.
87 Ibid.
88 Ibid., 128.
89 Ibid., 129.
90 Ibid., 131.
91 Ibid.
92 Ibid., 135.
93 Ibid., 137.
94 Ibid., 148.
95 Ibid., 151.
96 Ibid., 152.
97 Ibid., 154.
98 Ibid., 155.
99 Ibid., 156.
100 Ibid.
101 Editorial Note: Rabbi Hillel (1st Century BCE) was a hugely influential Jewish teacher. The quote is from the *Pirkei Avot*, I:14.
102 Nozick, *The Examined Life*, 158.
103 Ibid., 162.

104 Ibid., 165.
105 Ibid.
106 Ibid., 170.
107 Ibid., 171.
108 Ibid.
109 Ibid., 174.
110 Ibid., 177.
111 Ibid.
112 Ibid., 178.
113 Ibid.
114 *The Diaries of Franz Kafka 1910–1913*, ed. Max Brod, trans. Joseph Kresh (London: Secker & Warburg, 1948), 25.
115 Nozick, *The Examined Life*, 180.
116 Ibid.
117 Ibid., 181.
118 Ibid., 182.
119 Ibid., 184.
120 Ibid., 198.
121 Ibid., 198–9.
122 Ibid., 206.
123 Ibid., 205.
124 Ibid.
125 Ibid., 206.
126 Ibid., 207.
127 Ibid., 214.
128 Ibid.
129 Ibid., 215.
130 Ibid.
131 Ibid., 243.
132 Ibid., 244.
133 Ibid., 245.
134 Ibid., 246.
135 See Dilman, *Philosophy and the Philosophic Life*, Chapter 7, 'The Wheel of Time', 118–30.
136 Eugene O'Neill, *Long Day's Journey Into Night* (London: Jonathan Cape, 1966), 134–5.
137 Nozick, *The Examined Life*, 251.
138 O'Neill, *Long Day's Journey*, 134–5.

Closing Remarks

I have engaged with five individual works by different philosophers chosen at random. The experience was similar to visiting five different countries. Each work held in store different pleasures and irritations, but it also placed me in the company of a fellow philosopher. I have criticized my colleagues, which is part of philosophy; but I have also tried to appreciate them. What separates me from them is that I am not, and never have been, a 'philosopher's philosopher'; or, to put it differently, a 'professional philosopher', even though I am dedicated to philosophical reflection. I have taught philosophy all my working life, and taken my work seriously. In addition, I have written many books – and even more articles – on philosophical topics. You might say that I am a 'loner' in the field. I have been to philosophy conferences and read papers there; but I really work on my own.

I also think that I have turned a weakness into a strength. People always tell me that I write clearly. The reason why I do so is that I feel uneasy about moving too swiftly from one stage of an argument to the next. I have to tread slowly and be absolutely sure about what I think, etc. It is this that makes for my clarity, such as it is; it is, above all, clarity for myself.

I must also confess that, of the five authors I have discussed here, I have found John Searle and Philippa Foot to be the clearest. And while we disagree over a number of things, I have no other bone to pick with them. Dennett is a hybrid between scientist and philosopher. Since he is engrossed in philosophical materialism, we are pretty far apart. But again, when he raises an issue for discussion, he does so with a view to opening up new perspectives, and he does it well. Donald Davidson strikes me as 'too intellectual by half', as what I have called a 'philosopher's philosopher'. I find it more difficult to pass this kind of judgement on Robert Nozick because I suspect that *The Examined Life* is not a typical book of his. I mean this in the sense that the book consists of 'philosophical meditations'. But what strikes me about it is that it seems to reveal two distinct philosophical personalities. When Nozick writes, for example, about topics such as love, creativity, parenthood, dying, etc., he is clear, sensible, and insightful. At other times, he falls into seemingly meaning-less abstractions.

For this reason, I was greatly disappointed with Nozick's book. I had hoped that it would constitute a counterpoint to pedantic intellectualism. All I can say is that, in my view, decent philosophizing needs to keep a balance between two opposite extremes: it must keep its feet firmly and modestly on the ground and, *at the same time*, have the courage to let go of that ground, so that the familiar can assume a strange countenance. But it must be able to do this while maintaining its respect for language – not simply the language of the marketplace, but the different modes of language employed in talking about the diverse things we talk about, including the language of literature and poetry.

In all of this, one thing needs to be avoided like the plague: the so-called 'language of metaphysics'. I say 'so-called', because it is not a genuine language, does not have roots in any actual form of life. However, it is not always easy to distinguish between the language of metaphysics and the genuinely inventive language used by an outstanding philosopher. For instance, were Plato's 'Forms' metaphysical concepts? I think that, in talking of *Forms*, Plato was drawing a genuine and significant distinc-tion between concepts – or rather, he was singling out or setting apart concepts relevant to a range of philosophical problems. I have already argued that we find this distinction in Kant and in Wittgenstein, too, and cannot develop the point any further here. But we must remember that great philosophers, too, are susceptible to the lure of metaphysics, and that their analyses may combine metaphysics with genuine insight, all expressed with poetic licence.

We should also recall that where insight into religion has been expressed in poetic and mythological language, this has been interpreted as meta-physics. Those who have done so, have missed the real illumination, viz. the spiritual character of many religious beliefs. Similarly for the use of poetic and mythological language by the great philosophers of the past.

Finally, two further comments: (a) Like every other human creative activity, philosophy, too, is subject to fashion. Each philosopher is respon-sible for not giving in to its lure. This is a matter of the philosopher's individual character. He must certainly be open to, and learn from, others; but after an initial period of apprenticeship, he must make the problems he discusses his own, and what he says must come from him: he must have something to say. (I was going to add 'for himself', but that would be a pleonasm). Fashion designers can have something to say, too; their activity is an artistic one. Unfortunately, it preys on others; it encourages servility and mindlessness. In that sense, it is not an honourable profession.

(b) Philosophy, however much it encourages muddled thinking, is really an apprenticeship in clear thinking. One can learn to think clearly while reflecting on philosophical problems and being pulled into opposite directions at one and the same time. Personally, I not only learnt to think clearly and honestly – certainly, in philosophy the two go together – but to think about life, about its problems and their possible entanglements with philosophical problems. I believe I have now returned full circle to the point where I was drawn to philosophy in the first place, and that philosophy has helped me to learn about life. Obviously, one cannot acquire such learning from books, nor yet from reflection. But if one can learn to live in openness to life, then clear thinking and, indeed, philosophical thinking, can substantially contribute to a deepened understanding of life.

Bibliography

G. E. M. Anscombe, *Collected Philosophical Papers*. Vol. 3: *Ethics, Religion and Politics* (Minneapolis: University of Minnesota Press, 1981)

V. C. Chappell (ed.), *Philosophy of Mind* (Prentice-Hall: Englewood Cliffs, N.J., 1962)

R. Chisholm, *Freedom and Determinism*, ed. Keith Lehrer (New York: Random House, 1966)

Peter Clark and Crispin Wright (eds), *Mind, Psycho-Analysis and Science* (Oxford: Blackwell, 1988)

Donald Davidson, *Essays on Actions and Events* (Oxford: Clarendon Press, 1980)

Daniel Dennett, *Consciousness Explained* (London: Penguin, 1991)

Ilham Dilman, *Sense and Delusion* (London: Routledge & Kegan Paul, 1971)

—— *Induction and Deduction: A Study in Wittgenstein* (Oxford: Blackwell, 1973)

—— *Matter and Mind: Two Essays in Epistemology* (London: Macmillan, 1975)

—— *Morality and the Inner Life: A Study in Plato's 'Gorgias'* (London: Macmillan, 1979)

—— *Love and Human Separateness* (Oxford: Blackwell, 1987)

—— *Philosophy and the Philosophic Life* (London: Macmillan, 1992)

—— *Love: Its Forms, Dimensions and Paradoxes* (London: Macmillan, 1998)

—— *Free Will* (London: Routledge, 1999)

—— *Wittgenstein's Copernican Revolution* (London: Palgrave, 2000)

—— *Raskolnikov's Rebirth: Psychology and the Understanding of Good and Evil* (Chicago Ill.: Open Court, 2000)

—— *The Self, the Soul and the Psychology of Good and Evil* (London: Routledge, 2005)

Fyodor Dostoyevsky, *Crime and Punishment*, trans. Constance Garnett (London: Everyman, 1956)

Philippa Foot, *Natural Goodness* (Oxford: Clarendon Press, 2003)

P. T. Geach, *The Virtues* (Cambridge: Cambridge University Press, 1977)

Kahlil Gibran, *The Prophet* (Ware, Herts.: Wordsworth, 1966)

C. L. Hull, *Principles of Behavior* (New York: Appleton-Century-Crofts, 1943)

The Diaries of Franz Kafka 1910–1913, ed. Max Brod, trans. Joseph Kresh (London: Secker & Warburg, 1948)

Immanuel Kant, *Fundamental Principles of the Metaphysics of Morals*, trans. T. K. Abbot (London: Longman, Green and Co., 1909)

A. I. Melden, *Free Action* (London: Routledge & Kegan Paul, 1961)

Robert Nozick, *The Examined Life: Philosophical Meditations* (New York: Simon & Schuster, 1990)

Eugene O'Neill, *Long Day's Journey Into Night* (London: Jonathan Cape, 1966)

Plato, *Gorgias*, trans. Donald J. Zeyl, in *Plato: Complete Works*, ed. John M. Cooper (Indianapolis: Hackett, 1997)

Rainer Maria Rilke, *Sonnets to Orpheus*, trans. J. B. Leishman (London: Hogarth Press, 1936)

Jean-Paul Sartre, *L'Être et le néant* (Paris: Gallimard, 1943)

John Searle, *The Construction of Social Reality* (London: Penguin, 1995)

—— *Making the Social World* (Oxford: Oxford University Press, 2010)

Simone Weil, *Waiting for God*, trans. Emma Craufurd (New York: Harper & Row, 1973)

—— *Gravity and Grace*, trans. Emma Crawford (London: Routledge, 2002)

Peter Winch, *Ethics and Action* (London: Routledge, 1972)

John Wisdom, *Other Minds* (Oxford: Blackwell, 1952)

—— *Philosophy and Psycho-Analysis* (Oxford: Blackwell, 1953)

Ludwig Wittgenstein, *Tractatus Logico-Philosophicus*, trans. D. F. Pears and B. F. McGuinness (London: Routledge & Kegan Paul, 1969)

—— *Zettel*, ed. G. H. von Wright and G. E. M. Anscombe, trans. G. E. M. Anscombe (Oxford: Blackwell, 1981)

—— *Culture and Value*, 2nd Revised Edition, ed. G. H. von Wight, trans. Peter Winch (Oxford: Blackwell, 1998)

—— *On Certainty*, ed. G. E. M. Anscombe and G. H. von Wright, trans. Denis Paul and G. E. M. Anscombe (Oxford: Blackwell, 1998)

—— *Philosophical Investigations*, trans. G. E. M. Anscombe (Oxford: Blackwell, 1999)

Index